Street Computing

This book develops tools and techniques that will h
computing. Metaphorically speaking, it is taking
general public – rather than just researchers and
available city infrastructure and create solutions tail
together five articles that are based on presentation
shop held on 24 November 2009 in Melbourne in
puter-Human Interaction Conference (OZCHI 2009

This book focuses on applying urban informatic
open application programming interfaces (APIs) to t
online services, on demand and in real time. It then
Singapore has harnessed the potential of an onlin
visitors can access services electronically.

This book was published as a special issue of the

Marcus Foth is Associate Professor and a Principal
Design, and the Director of the Urban Informatics R
of Technology.

Markus Rittenbruch is a Senior Research Fellow with
at Queensland University of Technology.

Ricky Robinson is a Senior Research Scientist with N

Stephen Viller is a Senior Lecturer in the School of I
Engineering, University of Queensland.

Street Computing

Urban Informatics and City Interfaces

Edited by
Marcus Foth, Markus Rittenbruch, Ricky Robinson and Stephen Viller

Routledge
Taylor & Francis Group
LONDON AND NEW YORK

First published 2014
by Routledge
4 Park Square, Milton Park, Abingdon, Oxon OX14 4RN
605 Third Avenue, New York, NY 10017

Routledge is an imprint of the Taylor & Francis Group, an informa business

This book is a reproduction of *Journal of Urban Technology*, vol. 19, issue 2. The Publisher requests to those authors who may be citing this book to state, also, the bibliographical details of the special issue on which the book was based.

British Library Cataloguing in Publication Data
A catalogue record for this book is available from the British Library

ISBN13: 978-0-415-84336-2 (hbk)

Typeset in Minion
by Taylor & Francis Books

Publisher's Note
The publisher would like to make readers aware that the chapters in this book may be referred to as articles as they are identical to the articles published in the special issue. The publisher accepts responsibility for any inconsistencies that may have arisen in the course of preparing this volume for print.

Contents

Citation Information

The chapters in this book were originally published in the *Journal of Urban Technology*, volume 19, issue 2 (April 2012). When citing this material, please use the original page numbering for each article, as follows:

Chapter 1
Street Computing: Towards an Integrated Open Data Application Programming Interface (API) for Cities
Ricky Robinson, Markus Rittenbruch, Marcus Foth, Daniel Filonik and Stephen Viller
Journal of Urban Technology, volume 19, issue 2 (April 2012) pp. 1–24

Chapter 2
Designing for the Situated and Public Visualization of Urban Data
Andrew Vande Moere and Dan Hill
Journal of Urban Technology, volume 19, issue 2 (April 2012) pp. 25–46

Chapter 3
Probing Streets and the Built Environment with Ambient and Community Sensing
Flora Dilys Salim
Journal of Urban Technology, volume 19, issue 2 (April 2012) pp. 47–68

Chapter 4
User-Led Design in the Urban/Domestic Environment
Georgina Voss and Natasha Carolan
Journal of Urban Technology, volume 19, issue 2 (April 2012) pp. 69–88

Chapter 5
Enabling the Real-Time City: LIVE Singapore!
Kristian Kloeckl, Oliver Senn and Carlo Ratti
Journal of Urban Technology, volume 19, issue 2 (April 2012) pp. 89–112

Street Computing: Towards an Integrated Open Data Application Programming Interface (API) for Cities

Ricky Robinson, Markus Rittenbruch, Marcus Foth, Daniel Filonik and Stephen Viller

ABSTRACT *This special issue of the* Journal of Urban Technology *brings together five articles that are based on presentations given at the Street Computing Workshop held on 24 November 2009 in Melbourne in conjunction with the Australian Computer-Human Interaction conference (OZCHI 2009). Our own article introduces the Street Computing vision and explores the potential, challenges, and foundations of this research trajectory. In order to do so, we first look at the currently available sources of information and discuss their link to existing research efforts. Section 2 then introduces the notion of Street Computing and our research approach in more detail. Section 3 looks beyond the core concept itself and summarizes related work in this field of interest. We conclude by introducing the papers that have been contributed to this special issue.*

Introduction

The physical city is covered with an increasing number of layers of digital information. These rich sets of information are of increasing importance for decision-making processes in councils and local governments and open the possibility to a wide range of future applications and services which are the subject of intensified research efforts. While previous research endeavors have explored the creation of specialized tools to aid decision-making by urban citizens, councils and other stakeholders (Calabrese et al., 2009; Paulos et al., 2009), our vision goes a step further. We are aiming to address the challenge of helping people help themselves by enabling them to create their *own* decision support tools based upon urban data sources, civic sensor networks, and self-disclosed data (for example, from social networking applications). One of the main benefits of this is shifting the monitoring and processing burden from the user to the computational infrastructure.

The integration of information processing technologies into the environment is being investigated from several different perspectives that we discuss further below. However, our review shows that there is a lack of research dealing with the problem of making these information and computational capabilities accessible to everyday users. In order to address these challenges we introduce the notion of "Street computing" which draws heavily from the existing pool of research. "Street computing" tries to develop tools and techniques that will help users help themselves. Metaphorically speaking, it is taking computing to the street by giving the general public—rather than researchers and professionals—the power to leverage the available infrastructure and create solutions tailored to their individual needs. It is inspired by Corburn's "Street Science" in that it recognizes the imperative of local urban insights for improving scientific inquiry as well as policy and decision-making. Local involvement delivers crucial information for solving problems in urban communities and increases public trust, leading to a healthier political system (Corburn, 2005). Furthermore, by providing users with the right tools, Street computing enables citizens to take a more active role in the evolution of their cities and thereby reduces the burden placed on government services.

This special issue of the *Journal of Urban Technology* brings together five articles that are based on presentations given at the Street Computing Workshop held on 24 November 2009 in Melbourne in conjunction with the Australian Computer-Human Interaction conference (OZCHI 2009). Our own article introduces the street computing vision and explores the potential, challenges, and foundations of this research vision. In order to do so, we first look at the currently available sources of information and discuss their link to existing research efforts. Then we introduce the notion of street computing and our research approach in more detail. Finally, we look beyond the core concept itself and summarize related work in this field.

Sources of Information

In the context of our work, we consider three distinct sources of information—data gathered by sensors, information provided by public institutions, and social information created by social (mobile) applications. Hardware that enables sensing, computation, communication, and actuation is becoming smaller and cheaper to manufacture. The integration of these capabilities can be observed on various scales, from everyday objects to smart homes and urban environments. Through networking technologies, the individual building blocks are connected to form large systems with ever increasing complexity. Vast amounts of information are accumulated and processed in such systems. At the same time, we can observe a significant trend towards releasing public information. Recent "Government 2.0" and "Open Data" initiatives have led to the creation of public data catalogues that contain data such as flood maps, crime statistics, and location of facilities such as parks and public toilets. Last, but not least, the ubiquitous availability and increasing prevalence of social media applications provides access to a rich stream of user-generated content. The ubiquity and volume of this information together with the parallel trend towards incorporating location data into web and mobile applications are neatly summarized with the phrase: "The urbanization of the Internet, and the digitization of the city."

Sensing and Ubiquitous Computing

The diffusion of computational capacities into our surroundings is the subject of a number of research areas. Weiser laid the groundwork for ubiquitous computing in his article "The Computer for the Twenty-First Century" (1991). His vision called for seamless interaction between users and numerous small computers embedded in everyday objects. Weiser argues that such an approach would give users better access to existing and previously unavailable information. For Weiser, the integration of computers into the human environment is essential in order to allow users to interact with this information in a natural way. Consequently, he sees ubiquitous computing as a promising solution for the problem of information overload (Weiser, 1991). More recently, researchers have started to point out the disconnect between this envisioned future and the way technology has evolved. While ubiquitous computing has already become a reality "in the form of densely available computational and communication resources" (Bell and Dourish, 2007), the devices through which information is accessed are "highly present, visible, and branded" (Bell and Dourish, 2007). Nevertheless, a lot of research has been invested in developing technologies and applications that aim at making Weiser's vision a reality. The range of research topics is broad and covers a large scope of application areas. However, many of the projects limit themselves to "small-scale well-defined patches of the built environment such as smart houses or rooms" (Kindberg et al., 2007). In contrast to that, "urban computing" is a relatively recent area of research that looks at the impact of ubiquitous information processing at the scale of a city. The focus shifts from integrating computing into everyday objects towards everyday urban settings and lifestyles (Kindberg et al., 2007). Rather than formulating a particular vision for the future, urban computing aims to explore and understand the implications of emerging technologies on urban landscapes today (Paulos and Jenkins, 2005). Most importantly, it takes into account the complex and dynamic social interactions that take place in cities. Another research field revolving around the role of users is "participatory sensing," which looks at the potential of computational capabilities in the hands of the general public. Using everyday mobile devices, the goal is to "enable public and professional users to gather, analyze, and share local knowledge" (Burke et al., 2006). Unlike traditional distributed sensing, participatory sensing has to consider issues such as ensuring data credibility, protecting privacy, and encouraging participation (Burke et al., 2006). If these challenges are properly addressed, applications in this space hold the potential to engage and empower citizens in new ways (Paulos and Jenkins, 2005).

Open Data

Recent "Government 2.0" initiatives have led to the creation of public data repositories such as *data.gov* (United States), *data.gov.uk* (United Kingdom), and *data.gov.au* (Australia) on federal government levels; *datasf.org* (San Francisco), *data.london.gov.uk* (London), and *data.brisbane.qld.gov.au* (Brisbane) on municipal levels, and Transport for London (http://www.tfl.gov.uk/) and the San Francisco Metropolitan Transportation Commission (http://511.org) on the level of service providers, to name just a few. Data contained in these repositories ranges from data that is updated infrequently (e.g., public infrastructure) to real-time information (e.g., weather and flood warnings).[1] While some of this information was previously accessible through different services, the repositories fulfill two key functions. First, they centralize access to information by providing all information through a specific URL. Second, they simplify data access by providing data in a common format and provide a legal framework for the use of data.

Public data is commonly released in a number of formats. These include generic file formats such as CSV, as well as data-specific formats such as DWG and KML for data relating to geographical information systems and maps. In addition to these pre-existing formats, there are a number of protocols specifically designed for open data (e.g., http://www.odata.org/) as well as frameworks that allow public institutions to easily host and publish open data (e.g., http://ckan.org/). Orthogonal to these technical concerns of data storage and dissemination are legal frameworks designed to govern the use and licensing of public sector information. Creative Commons (CC) licenses, such as "CC Attribution 3.0"[2] simplify data access and licensing issues.

Social Mobile Information

The ubiquitous availability of social media applications provides access to a stream of user-generated content that includes reviews, feedback, opinions, and reporting of incidents, such as traffic incidents, municipal repair requests (e.g., Foth et al., 2011), and emergency information. While individual applications serve specific purposes, it is the mining of various social media streams that allows developers to tap into a rich set of interrelated user-generated information.

The Street Computing Approach

In the following section we describe our vision for a broad set of research subsumed under the term "street computing." We have begun to implement parts of this vision and are aiming to implement further research projects in this area with our partners in local government and industry.

We exemplify our research approach by considering the problem of urban mobility. We are interested in determining how people currently make decisions concerning their daily travel plans, and how their *in situ* decision-making might be improved if they could construct highly personalized travel planners by combining public transport timetables, real-time traffic updates, ride-sharing information, social network data, personal and office calendar, and any other information deemed relevant by that individual.

In decision-making for daily travel, several common practices can be observed. Commuters use web-based trip planners offered by public transport providers, who may also offer a version that can be accessed on a mobile phone. Some of these providers also offer real-time information on their web sites and at bus/train stations. People will often print out timetables to put on their walls for reference. Furthermore, they may tune into traffic reports on the radio to keep up with traffic incidents which may influence their choice of transport mode. Recently, some public transport providers have begun to use services such as Twitter to make announcements about cancelled services, track work on railways, and so on. Twitter has also been used for "crowd-sourcing" traffic incidents.[3] Finally, personal events recorded in calendars or diaries must also be consulted, often for the purpose of putting hard bounds on arrival time at the destination. These non-provider sources of information play a large part in decision-making, and illustrate that the process of travel planning is different for each person.

One limitation with current practices is the necessity for commuters to monitor all of these various information sources and combine them in their heads. A second limitation is that existing technology solutions to travel-planning take a provider-centric view rather than a commuter-centric one, meaning that commuters are offered trip planning tools that are not tailored to their individual needs and circumstances. Note that merely having access to real-time information about bus and train arrival times does not solve this problem.

The state-of-the-art in trip planning is the Personal Travel Assistant (CUD, 2009) from Cisco and its partners in the *Connected Urban Development* program, which does endeavor to provide a personalized decision support tool. However, it is limited in that users cannot add their own information sources (such as calendar information) to the tool. Furthermore, the solution is specific to urban travel, rather than a general platform that can underpin solutions to many problems in the urban realm.

We are interested in exploring end-user programming techniques that enable users to construct their own decision support tools. However, our solution is general and will have many applications beyond the problem of urban mobility that is being considered here. There are three major elements to our approach: interaction techniques for end-user composition; a framework for composition; and the urban computing substrate.

Interaction Techniques for End-User Composition

There are numerous examples of end-user programming, ranging from simple but inflexible approaches to more sophisticated techniques that are still beyond the grasp of the lay user. We outline some of these approaches here, moving from the simple to the more complex:

- setting the time or recording schedule on a VCR or PVR (personal video recorder). The task has been simplified with the advent of G-codes—a short numerical code representing a TV program that can be typed into the VCR or PVR
- programming-by-example in desktop applications such as the Microsoft Office suite, whereby the user "records" a sequence of actions so that this sequence can be invoked in a single step at a later time. A generated script in a high-level language is often used to represent the sequence
- repetitive tasks in desktop environments can be automated with the use of tools such as Apple OS X Automator, in which users compose a workflow from a set of actions that can be linked together. In the same spirit, but for a different purpose, we are beginning to see tools to simplify the task of creating "mash-ups" from web-based data. Tools such as Intel MashMaker[4] and Yahoo Pipes[5] fall into this category.

While end-user programming has been shown to be feasible for customizing personal spaces (Chin et al., 2006a), creating video/audio capture and access tools for the home (Truong et al., 2004) and configuring home multimedia systems (Newman et al., 2008), our approach is to create an experience resembling something that most people are already familiar with: meal preparation. Just as people go shopping for ingredients that they bring home to combine in a particular way to create a meal for themselves, our approach involves visually exposing data and computational elements in the physical world, which can be "gathered" by ordinary people, and then combined by them in a specific way to achieve something that is personally or socially meaningful.

In contrast to existing end-user approaches to combining data and processing, our approach, which we term "conceptual composition," is:

Situated. Users carry with them the context within which a computational element was captured, which serves as an aid to the user at the time of composition.

Physical. We want to provide users with an experience similar to that of meal preparation, which deals in physical objects.

User-Centered. Our approach considers the manner in which users approach similar tasks. For example, trial and error is one strategy commonly deployed by people in trying to achieve a particular result from a combination of elements (in cooking, for instance), and so it follows that we should investigate how our solution can support such behavior. Other less obvious constraints and behaviors will be discovered via a set of user studies that underpin our approach.

In the urban mobility use case, this approach might be realized by embedding symbolic representations of components (such as bus timetables and real-time traffic information) in the environment, and to enable users to "capture" the elements on their mobile devices for later use in a composition. Initially, these symbols might be unique identifiers such as QR codes. Later, and depending upon our findings from user studies, we may evolve this capture technique to use object recognition in combination with augmented reality, so that components can be identified on the screen of a mobile phone as one walks around, and then "dragged" into a composition or onto a clipboard for later use.

A Framework for Composition

The proposed framework integrates tightly with both the interaction techniques for end-user composition and the computing substrate below it.

The composition framework maps the user-specified composition to an executable representation and oversees the (distributed) execution of the composition. However, the framework will also support directly programmed applications, which might be developed by a skilled engineer as opposed to an end-user. In this sense it is analogous to a web development framework such as Django[6] or Ruby on Rails,[7] or a toolkit for context-aware computing (Dey et al., 2001; Henricksen and Indulska, 2006).

Unlike web development frameworks, an underlying network of dynamic data sources (that is, the urban computing substrate, described below) rather than relational databases will back the applications. Furthermore, the processing and rendering components of a composition may be executed locally or remotely according to need and environmental constraints, for example, does the local environment have an appropriate device or public display for rendering visuals?

We will explore several different techniques for mapping user-specified compositions into executable code. One possibility is that the graphical or tangible objects exposed to end-users are tied directly to corresponding software objects within the framework, and workflow creation then becomes a matter of traditional object-oriented composition. Another approach is to use meta-programming, in which the end-user compositions generate program *closures* within the framework, which can be executed by the local framework instance, or sent to one or more remote sites (i.e., in the cloud). We will see that the latter approach is consistent with the proposed architecture of the urban substrate. Because one or more remote machines may execute the composition, the generated code should be expression-limited.

Motivated by the urban mobility use case, we use the framework to explore the concept of "smart" compositions through a "significant places" learner (Hightower et al., 2005; Kim et al., 2009; Lane et al., 2008; Zhou et al., 2007), and an extension called "significant situations:" re-occurring situations that hold subjective meaning for an individual or group. This investigation of significant situations is more difficult than the creation of the framework itself in terms of implementation and the range of second order challenges that flow from it.

We assume that significant situations may be predicated upon arbitrary components or higher order compositions, selected or created by the end user. We will explore a number of approaches to situation learning and recognition. Brdiczka, Crowley, and Reignier (2007) employ Hidden Markov Models (HMM) to "learn" situations, which are updated with user feedback. However, their work does not relate to end-user programming or decision-support tools; rather it relates specifically to context-aware service selection, whereby particular services are invoked in particular situations. Other candidates include Bayesian networks, Dempster-Shafer Theory, and Support Vector Machines, some of which have been employed previously in the closely related task of context reasoning (Bettini et al., 2010).

Leveraging the early work of Lane et al. (2008), we also want to investigate the potential to share data and models among people within the same social network to improve the performance of our recognition algorithms. To this end we will attempt to derive an ontological basis upon which to formulate an understanding of situation models. In other words, is it possible to determine whether two or more situation models, independently specified (via conceptual composition) and trained by different people, are equivalent, or related in some other way (subsumption, for instance), such that we can decide whether or not to share models and/or training data among users?

Given a formal basis for the sharing of models, we are obliged to consider the privacy implications for such sharing. In practice, there will be a trade-off between improved user experience through superior situation recognition and privacy. A related question is under what circumstances an inference can be disclosed to other users, that is, if a situation is recognized, who must/should/must not be notified? Drawing upon existing work in privacy control (for example Boyle and Greenberg, 2005; Palen and Dourish, 2003; Wishart et al., 2005), we will investigate how obfuscation can be applied to the underlying data or the user interface to reduce the resolution of situation recognition. For instance, an ontological model of significant situations will enable the disclosure of coarser grained situation information in the case where the finer grained situation (say, "waiting at the bus stop on Moggill Road") is subsumed by a coarser grained one ("somewhere in suburb X").

The Urban Computing Substrate

The urban computing substrate is the collection of computational and data elements together with the protocols that underpin the above. Current architectures for distributed data-driven applications generally follow one of two approaches (Henricksen and Robinson, 2006). Middleware for sensor networks take a bottom-up approach that starts with the capabilities and constraints of the hardware platform and endeavors to provide software engineering abstractions that assist with extracting data from the network without requiring application developers to deal with low-level hardware and networking issues. An alternative is the top-down approach, in which a deep understanding of application requirements is a primary driver for the design of the middleware. To some extent, this is the approach that has been taken in the field of context-aware computing.

What is now required is a converged approach, which lends itself to the sophisticated high-level programming and query abstractions typical of context-aware computing environments, as well as the distributed execution environments offered by middleware for sensor networks. Coupled with the framework described above, our substrate will provide the execution environment and messaging primitives to realize the conceptual compositions defined by end-users and developers. To this end, we propose an architecture that is similar in style to Computational REST (Erenkrantz et al., 2007), or CREST, which advocates computation rather than content as the fundamental unit of transfer.

However, CREST is silent on publish/subscribe models of communication, which are prevalent in the literature on middleware for sensor networks and context-aware computing due to the loose coupling they afford (that is, subscribers need not have any knowledge of the identity and location of publishers), and which are desirable in real-time decision support systems. We, therefore, explore asynchronous extensions to CREST, to enable scalable, selective, real-time updates from streaming data sources or lower order compositions. In particular, we investigate computational subscriptions and notifications. That is, in keeping with CREST philosophy, subscriptions and notifications will be executable code (closures), meaning, for example, that publishers can export the processing overhead due to data conversion from one format to another to the subscriber (a generally more scalable approach) or any intermediary host, and that the subscriber need not be pre-programmed with the particular data conversion algorithm. A further use for this architectural style is that notifications may simply be pointers to other computations or data instead of containing the data itself, and the client application need not have any knowledge that this is the case. Figure 1 depicts the different components of our research approach.

Individualized Data Stream Composition and Visualization

We have started to implement some aspects of the larger research vision of Street Computing. We have developed an iPad application that supports individualized data stream compositions and visualizations, in the form of a dashboard that allows users to easily combine and display different types of data sources. The application is aimed at individual home users and allows access to data sources such as home energy data (e.g., through Pachube, now renamed: Cosm) and social media data. The project acknowledges that individual users have different preferences with regard to the style in which they want to present certain data (e.g., graph vs. smiley face animation for energy data) and with regard to which data they want to display at the same time. While the dashboard does not yet

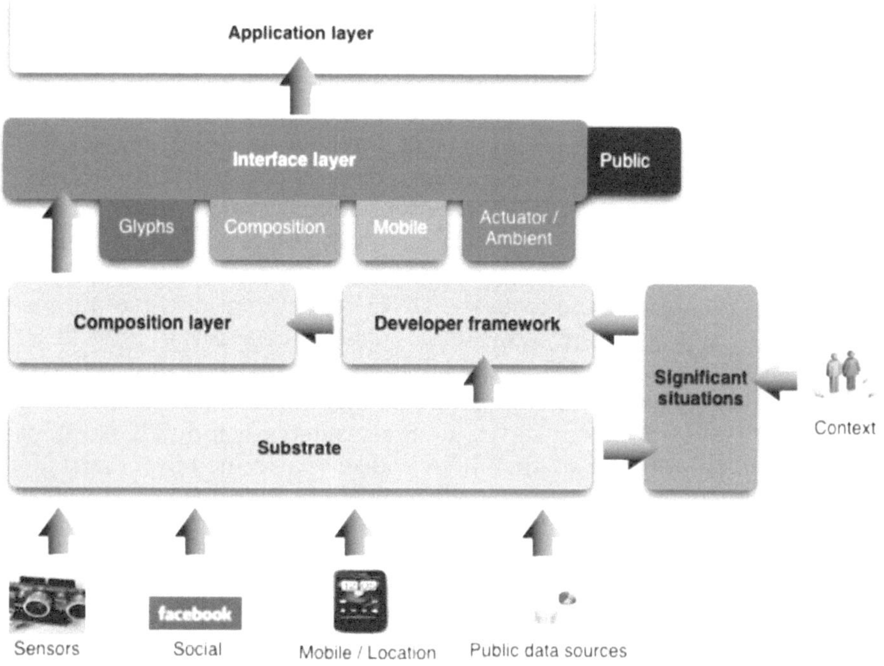

Figure 1: Integrated Open Data API – Components

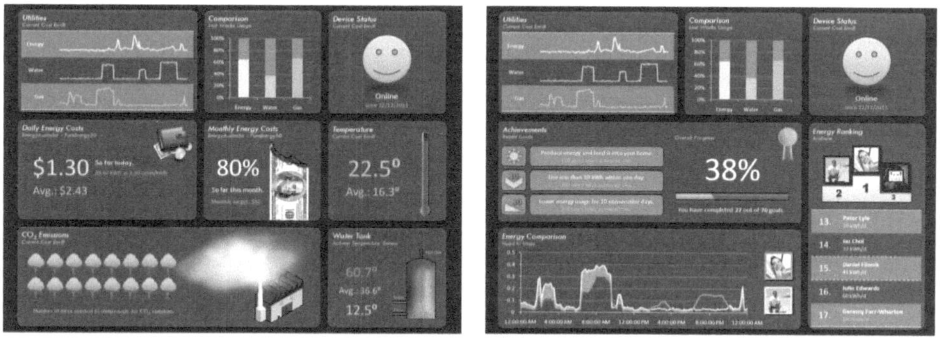

Figure 2: Dashboard Mockups

support full data integration, it is a first step in exploring the individualization of data streams. Figure 2 displays some of the current mockups.

Related Works

The following section presents the major challenges and open research questions in the area of street computing. These issues were identified by reviewing literature from related research areas and analyzing projects that are positioned in this particular space. This review aims to point out reoccurring problems and group them so they can be addressed in future research.

Integrating Heterogeneous Data Sources

Already today, our urban environments are monitored and analyzed through distributed computing and communication technologies. Complex and mostly independent systems support our everyday activities in the city, such as public transportation, mobile communication, and financial services. Further, various corporate and government entities collect data about traffic, pollution, and weather. It is foreseeable that this computing environment will incorporate an even wider variety of devices and services from different manufacturers and developers. In order to accomplish the goal of making this wealth of information from urban systems accessible to users, street computing needs to address the issue of working with heterogeneous data sources. Therefore, to provide a solid foundation for future projects, it is crucial to achieve platform and vendor independence, as well as architecture openness (Lee et al., 2007).

Zambonelli envisions those separate urban systems as individual organs that can "collaboratively contribute capabilities and services aimed to support increasing quality of life levels" (Zambonelli, 2011: 582). He advocates the development of proper collaboration and middleware tools that allow "all the components of the infrastructure ... dynamically and adaptively connect and collaborate with each other" (Zambonelli, 2011: 578). Such tools would greatly simplify the development of applications for street computing. Currently, most projects resort to creating this functionality from scratch, investing considerable time and effort. Providing adequate solutions to this challenge would benefit scientific progress by allowing researchers to focus on other questions that lie beyond.

For instance, the *Weave* architecture is one specific effort to develop standard APIs for services offered by sensing fabrics. Its goal is to simplify the design of applications across heterogeneous sensor networks that are independently managed. It recognizes that it is often necessary for applications in urban sensing to "fuse information from sensing fabrics extant in the environment, to meet requirements for which the fabrics were not designed a priori" (Kulathumani et al., 2008: 1). The work distinguishes between a generic API for urban sensing and vertical APIs specific to application domains. The architecture is put to the test by focusing on the domain of search applications and applying it to concrete scenarios (Kulathumani et al., 2008).

While it may not be feasible or even desirable to try and formulate an all-encompassing generic standard for urban computing—given the wide variety of application domains and problems—it would be helpful to have guidelines and best practices that manufacturers and developers can follow. Certain aspects can certainly be abstracted, such as the protocols for publishing and subscribing to data streams. However, even with a successful attempt at standardization, it is still necessary to have ways of integrating legacy and non-conformant systems.

Extracting Information and Knowledge

As the technologies for gathering data are widely deployed within urban areas, including smart homes, the leading question becomes how to process the collected data. The relationship among data, information, and knowledge is explored in information systems and knowledge management literature. That relationship is often represented as a hierarchy in which the higher levels are increasingly rich with meaning. While this concept is generally agreed upon, there is less consensus about "the processes that transform elements lower in the hierarchy into those above them" (Rowley, 2007: 7). According to the classical definition by Ackoff, knowledge allows us to apply data and information to give answers to questions of "how" (Ackoff, 1989). Such questions lie at the core of the problems that urban communities face, for example: "How do we reduce traffic congestion?" "How do we support healthy and sustainable lifestyles?" or "How do we plan and develop neighborhoods with a high quality of life?"

Comprehensive ontologies suitable for urban computing are a critical prerequisite for applying semantic technologies. In turn, these technologies hold enormous potential for street computing by semantically interpreting the sensor output and thereby allowing non-technical users to benefit from data that would otherwise be meaningless to them. In the design of the search API for the *Weave* architecture proposed by Kulathumani et al. (2008) sensor fabrics are viewed as providers of an extensible database of "query-able" objects. As part of their future work, the authors aim to extend the search functionality to enable queries with richer semantics. In order to accomplish this goal, they plan to develop "a richer ontology for urban sensing that builds up from physical phenomena, sensing signatures, detectors, and richer classes of objects" (Kulathumani et al., 2008: 7).

Effective decision-support systems require actionable information and knowledge about the situation in question. In order to provide this information, algorithms need to be developed that can combine static knowledge about the urban environment with the dynamic data streams originating from sensors. Della Valle et al. (2008) propose a system that adapts reasoning techniques to work with the resulting time-varying knowledge. Their solution combines semantic reasoners with throughput-efficient data stream management systems (Della Valle et al., 2008).

The *Semantic Streams* framework by Whitehouse et al. (2006) presents another approach that supports the quick extraction of semantic information from sensor output. The framework is based on a declarative language for specifying and composing inference units that are "minimal units of sensor data interpretation" (Whitehouse et al., 2006: 5). Existing inference units can be dynamically composed to generate new interpretations of sensor data. This allows non-technical users to pose queries over semantic interpretations of sensor data without having to write code performing the inference themselves (Whitehouse et al., 2006).

Supporting Mashups and End-User Programming

An area that is still largely unexplored in the context of urban computing is the potential for end-user programming. This aspect is a fundamental part of street computing and its vision of empowering users. Making it possible for the general public to leverage the existing technical infrastructure and create solutions tailored to their individual needs requires the development of new tools and techniques. A user-centric approach is necessary to make the available functionality easy to understand and use.

The issue of end-user programming can be addressed from several different directions. There is substantial room for improvement when it comes to querying the sensing environment. Users need better ways of retrieving the information relevant to their individual problems. Query languages based on semantic interpretations of sensor data permit a more natural way of inquiry by allowing the use of high-level concepts. This relieves the user of the burden of making low-level decisions based on the raw sensor data. Such an approach has the additional benefit of introducing an extra degree of freedom to the system. The user does not specify what exact sensor data is used and how it is processed to infer the desired information (Whitehouse et al., 2006).

Another means of approaching end-user programming is through the composition of existing data and services. This has recently come to the center of research in the realm of web services, where such compositions are referred to as mash-ups. Several different paradigms of end-user programming have been explored with regards to creating mash-ups. Among those are simplified domain-specific languages, programming-by-example, and visual programming based on the data flow metaphor. The latter is a rather prominent paradigm that has been employed in several commercial implementations, such as *Microsoft Popfly* or *Yahoo!Pipes*. In this approach, the composition is represented as a graph of components, each of which has input and output parameters. A component transforms the data received in the input parameters and stores the result in the output parameters. By creating connections, the output parameters of one component act as input parameters of another, resulting in a design pattern similar to the pipeline or pipe and filter technique popularized by Unix command-line shells (Biörnstad and Pautasso, 2007; Wong and Hong, 2007).

The *SensorMasher* platform is one specific example for adapting the concept of mash-ups to sensing environments. It specifies how to publish sensors on the web and access their associated data through URIs. Further, it provides ways of linking these published entities to ontological concepts. This information is used in the visual composer to provide an intuitive interface for navigating and exploring sensor data sources by following semantic links. Once the user finds the relevant sensor data sources, he can use the work flow editor to visually combine the data and apply data processing operators. The resulting mash-up can be published and put to work in subsequent compositions (Le-Phuoc and Hauswirth, 2009).

Further research is necessary to explore ways for users to control the ubiquitous computational capabilities that form the basis for street computing. Chin et al. extend programming-by-example to a ubiquitous computing context by allowing users to "show" the system the desired behavior "via natural physical interaction with the environment" (Chin et al., 2006b: 325). The system deduces rules based on the actions that users perform with the physical devices themselves or with the corresponding interface elements. Beyond that, other approaches incorporate tangible user interfaces to represent key programming concepts in the course of the interaction between the user and his surroundings (Chin et al., 2006b; Hague et al., 2003).

Interfaces Supporting Composition

One of the challenges of developing interactive technologies for the urban environment is the diversity of interaction technologies, modalities, and settings in which the interaction takes place. In order to support composition of programming in-the-wild, we need to understand both interaction mechanisms and available technologies as well as the specific use context people operate in.

A large body of research in ubiquitous computing and human-computer interaction has laid the groundwork for understanding how computing can be manifested in a post-desktop world. We will focus on three major aspects: mobile interfaces, ambient and situated interaction, and novel interaction techniques such as gesture-based and organic user interfaces.

Post-Desktop and Urban Interfaces. The now near-pervasive availability of mobile devices[8] has opened the door to new types of interactions and services. The notion of location and location-based services lie at the very heart of ubiquitous computing research. Researchers in this field have explored services ranging from electronic city guides (e.g., Cheverst et al., 2000; Paay et al., 2009), education (e.g., Underwood et al., 2008), location-based games (e.g., Benford et al., 2004), to location-based notification systems for police officers (e.g., Streefkerk et al., 2008). There is a growing number of commercially available social mobile applications that use location data to maintain social networks (e.g., Foursquare, Google Latitude, Brightkite, Plazes, Fire Eagle, Zkout, and Rummble) and predict social trends (e.g., CitySense).[9]

An important development in this context is the use of augmented reality in combination with mobile devices in order to overlay a city with an additional interactive information layer. For instance, iCam (Patel et al., 2006), a location and orientation aware device, has been used to demonstrate the annotation of real-world objects (without the necessity of static labels). Metro Paris Subway[10] is an iPhone application that overlays real-world environments with additional information enabling service discovery and way showing. (See Figure 3.)

While personal mobile devices have been the predominant platform for interaction away from the desktop in recent years, ambient and situated displays play a

Figure 3: Metro Paris Subway
Source: <http://www.metroparisiphone.com/images/photos/9.jpg>

similarly important role in Mark Weiser's vision of ubiquitous computing. Advances in interaction technology, like the availability of large-scale multi-touch wall displays have led to an increased deployment of interactive displays in urban environments. CityWall is a large multi-touch interactive display installed in Helsinki that displays information about events happening in the city. Peltonen et al. (2008) studied how large interactive displays get shared and addressed issues such as crowding, teamwork, and conflict management, as well as the questions of how content from personal mobile devices get shared on public displays (Peltonen et al., 2007). The MIT SENSEable City Lab has designed an interactive bus stop that is targeted for a large-scale rollout in Florence, Italy. (See Figure 4.) These EyeStop[11] stations will allow users to interact with bus locations, timetables, bus proximity, community boards, route plotting functions, and advertisements. In addition, there is an increasing amount of research into non-standard urban interfaces such as urban pixels (Seitinger et al., 2009) or façade interactions (Dalsgaard and Halskov, 2010).

While each of the services and technologies discussed here represent interesting approaches to interacting with information away from the desktop, they focus on isolated modes of interaction. The EyeStop concept goes further in that it combines different display technologies (e.g., E-ink and LED displays) with different modes of interaction (web-browsing, timetables, ambient displays, etc.). Our approach differs from the above in that we are seeking to develop a platform that grants users access to the underlying layer of information and allows them to not only compose their own application, but also to use existing public input and output mechanisms available in the city environment.

Interaction Techniques for Composability. Tangible computing has been shown to be successful in a wide range of situations, including early learning: e.g., *Token Bowl*

Figure 4: EyeStop by the MIT SENSEable City Lab
Source: <http://senseable.mit.edu/eyestop/01.jpg>

Figure 5: Reactable
Source: <http://www.reactable.com/images/live2_design1.jpg>

(Martinussen et al., 2007), *jabberstamp* (Raffle et al., 2007), and *FlowBlocks* (Zuckerman et al., 2006); editing media content, e.g., *Mediablocks* (Ullmer and Ishii, 1999); disaster planning, e.g., the *Tangible Disaster Simulation System* (Ben-Joseph et al., 2001); and urban planning, e.g., *Urp* (Underkoffler and Ishii, 1999) and *Illuminating Clay* (Piper et al, 2002). Tangible User Interfaces (TUIs) couple physical representation with digital representation (Ullmer and Ishii, 2000). TUIs are particularly suited to the tasks of composition as physical objects are used as handles for virtual objects, e.g., *Bricks* (Fitzmaurice et al., 1995). Virtual objects are modified by manipulating corresponding physical objects (moving, shaking, orientating, exerting pressure, etc.). Composition of physical objects is a common task in TUIs and has been explored in many contexts, for instance musical composition (Jordà et al., 2007) and building simple programs through sensor network user interfaces (Merrill et al., 2007).

With regard to composability, we argue that the combination of tangible computing with surface or touch-based computing can provide an intuitive, natural interaction between the computer and the human during the application development phase. The *Reactables* (See Figure 5) are an example of such an approach because they combine tangible objects with touch-based interaction (multi-touch) on a tabletop surface (Jordà et al., 2007). However, unlike the *Reactable* where the display is mainly used to represent visual feedback on the immediate interaction, the street computing approach requires the visualization of a wider range of information related to specific sensors, services including maps, environmental data, contextualized sensor data, and computational elements such as data filters and aggregators. We envisage that this will allow users and developers to explore and simulate the implication of different combinations as part of the process of creating compositions.

Contributing and Sharing Resources

Street computing aims to develop systems that allow the general public to make use of distributed computational resources to gather information about urban environments. At the same time, the public should be encouraged to contribute resources at their disposal. With increased availability of resources, the potential applications of the system become broader. However, resources may be exclusive or constrained, making it necessary to coordinate access and resolve conflicts. For example, if a user chooses to supply his mobile device as a sensor, battery life would be a resource limiting how the sensing is carried out.

In order to design a system that relies on collaboration and sharing, it is essential to understand the factors that motivate people to participate. For certain users, the driving force might be seeing how their data contribute to a larger whole. In other cases it may be necessary to identify and design novel interaction mechanisms to provide incentives for participation (Cuff et al., 2008; Zambonelli, 2011). Taking resource constraints into account, one viable approach might be to grant preferred access to those users who also contribute to the system.

The problem of limited shared resources in urban sensing systems has been addressed in different research projects. It becomes especially relevant if the systems provide end-user programming capabilities, which are inherent in street computing. The *CitySense* project is one such example. In order to tackle this issue, resources are exposed through a custom API, which serves the purpose of restricting the programming model and allowing the underlying framework to perform optimizations such as caching (Murty et al., 2008).

Another approach for distributing load and resolving resource conflicts is taken by Whitehouse et al. and their *Semantic Streams* framework. The declarative specification language provides the capability of defining the quality of service trade-offs. Their framework uses this information together with its semantic inference capabilities to dynamically select the best available resources for answering a particular query (Whitehouse et al., 2006).

Providing Security and Privacy

Sharing and collaboration are fundamental components of street computing. Its applications can only thrive in an environment where users are encouraged to participate and feel comfortable exchanging data. Individual contributions of local and domain-specific knowledge are key to solving complex problems in urban communities. In order to facilitate such an exchange, it is crucial to have fully-fledged privacy and security mechanisms in place.

The data that drives street computing poses some unique challenges in terms of privacy. It has a high potential for revealing personal information, "because urban sensing collects information in environments inhabited by and directly connected to human beings" (Cuff et al., 2008: 30). From mobile devices to cars or smart homes, users carry sensors on their bodies or have them installed on their property. As a result, sensing device custodians are engaging in constant self-surveillance. Furthermore, this monitoring may compromise the privacy of those who are not custodians or primary sensing targets—an effect that Campbell et al. liken to "second-hand smoke" (2008: 16). Finally, the collected data may reveal information that goes beyond the original purpose of the sensing system (Campbell et al., 2008; Cuff et al., 2008). Adams and Sasse aptly summarize this problem, stating that "most invasions of privacy are not intentional but due to designers' inability to anticipate how this data could be used, by whom, and how this might affect users" (2001: 49).

Given the sensitivity of the information, it is unlikely that users will participate in street computing if they do not trust the underlying systems. One aspect of establishing trust is putting the users in charge of their personal data. This includes providing ways to control how personal data are collected, distributed, and processed. When sharing their data, users should have an option to become anonymous or pseudonymous and select the level of data granularity (Cuff et al., 2008). Designing usable and effective user-interfaces for controlling privacy and security capabilities is challenging. One major reason is that "users value and want security and privacy functionality, but they regard this functionality as secondary to completing their primary tasks" (Karat et al., 2005: 2). Therefore, additional research in the area of human-computer interaction is necessary to develop solutions that deliver a better user experience (Karat et al., 2005).

Different approaches have been proposed that allow people to make contributions to urban data collection efforts while providing strong individual privacy. One such solution is *PriSense*, which is based on data slicing and mixing and supports a wide range of statistical aggregation functions. Instead of directly answering a query, sensor nodes split their data into slices and pass them to randomly chosen cover nodes where they are mixed. From the responses of the different nodes, the initiator of the request can calculate an accurate aggregation result (Shi et al., 2010). A different approach is taken by *PoolView*, which is based on data perturbation. The idea is to make it impossible to reconstruct an individual data sequence's items or their trend without large error, while at the same time allowing to estimate the community data distribution and the average community data trend with high accuracy (Ganti et al., 2008). The *MetroSense* project is addressing privacy issues by "providing sensing device custodians with a notion of anonymity through k-anonymous tasking" (Campbell et al., 2008: 16; Cornelius et al., 2008).

Conclusion

One of the most profound changes to our world in recent times is the urbanization of society. Since mid-2007, the majority of humankind lives in urban centers (Tibaijuka, 2008: 1–2), but this is only the beginning: a report from McKinsey and Company (2009) predicts that China alone will build 20,000 to 50,000 skyscrapers over the next twenty years; this is equivalent to ten current-day New York Cities. Australia is at the forefront of this global megatrend: it is forecast that by 2015, nearly 90 percent of Australia's population will dwell in urban areas (UNDP, 2008). These changes bring with them many challenges. Existing urban problems, including traffic congestion, pollution, stress on civic services, incidence of crime, etc. will intensify correspondingly (for the correlation between population size and crime volume and rate, e.g., see Nolan III, 2004). Yet the increasing population in cities affords numerous opportunities for research in the social sciences, architecture, urban planning and, of course, ICT. The street computing project sits squarely in this space and is uniquely positioned to produce significant results and have tangible impacts.

Rather than trying to develop this research agenda in isolation and with limited or non-disclosure contained within a single research lab, our aim right from the start has been to apply the "street" philosophy not only to the technology, but to our development approach itself. For this reason, we organized early on the aforementioned Street Computing Workshop at OZCHI 2009 and shared our vision with like-minded colleagues working in the fields of urban informatics, human-computer interaction, and ubiquitous computing, and in turn encouraged them to share their own aspirations and related projects. We believe that this mutual exchange of works-in-progress will help build momentum around an internationally significant and collaborative research agenda for urban technology and urban informatics. This special issue has been guest edited with this spirit in mind.

We are pleased that four teams of colleagues followed our invitation to revise their workshop submissions into full, peer-reviewed articles for this special issue of the *Journal of Urban Technology*. These contributions allow us to present and discuss broader aspects of the street computing agenda from multiple perspectives. Andrew Vande Moere and Dan Hill focus on urban data visualizations. They introduce case studies that are based on both academic research projects as well as experimental design studios in order to postulate a set of design constraints for situated and public visualization of urban data. Flora Salim argues that conventional ways of interrogating specific buildings or urban projects are often inadequate to deliver the micro-scale granularity required at this scale. She discusses the capacity of urban probes to conduct ambient and community sensing of environmental, behavioral, or socio-cultural data that can inform urban design decisions. Georgina Voss and Natasha Carolan introduce the "Homesense" project which aims to bridge the gap between urban and domestic spaces as well as between purely technical and situated ("lived") expertise. The study initiated a participatory design approach for the user-led development of "open hardware toolkits" that were used as cultural probes. Finally, Kristian Kloeckl, Oliver Senn, and Carlo Ratti of the SENSEable City Lab at MIT present the *LIVE Singapore!* project. As far as we can tell, this project has the closest resemblance with the street-computing vision, but with a focus on open data initiatives such as those that emerged from the Government 2.0 movement. *LIVE Singapore!* promises to become an open platform that developers interested in the City of Singapore can use to create innovative mash-ups of an increasing amount of urban data streams.

Acknowledgments

This study is supported by the Queensland Government, which awarded a Smart Futures Fellowship to Marcus Foth, and by National ICT Australia (NICTA). Further support has been received from the Queensland Department of Environment and Resource Management, Current Cost, Smart Now Pty Ltd, and the Apple University Consortium, Australia. We would like to thank Petromil Petkov, Richard Medland, Margot Brereton, Iain Scott, Ronald Schroeter, Carlo Ratti, and Derek Foster for valuable advice, feedback, and technical support.

Note on Contributors

Ricky Robinson is a researcher at the Queensland Research Laboratory of National ICT Australia (NICTA).

Markus Rittenbruch is a senior research fellow with the Urban Informatics Research Lab, School of Design, Queensland University of Technology.

Marcus Foth is the director of the Urban Informatics Research Lab, and principal research fellow in the School of Design, Queensland University of Technology.

Daniel Filonik is a research intern at the Urban Informatics Research Lab, Queensland University of Technology, completing his computer science degree at Ludwig-Maximilians-Universität, München, Germany.

Stephen Viller is a senior lecturer in the School of Information Technology & Electrical Engineering, University of Queensland.

Notes

1. <http://opendata-tools.org/> provides a comprehensive overview of many of these repositories
2. <http://creativecommons.org/licenses/by/3.0/au/deed.en>
3. See, for example, SAP Research's iPhone app AUS Traffic, and the #bnetraffic hashtag on Twitter
4. <http://mashmaker.intel.com/>
5. <http://pipes.yahoo.com/>
6. <http://www.djangoproject.com/>
7. <http://rubyonrails.org/>
8. The Australian mobile penetration rate is predicted to reach 122 percent by 2012 (ITWire http://www.itwire.com/content/view/18424/1231/ Accessed December 21, 2011).
9. <http://www.citysense.com/>
10. <http://www.metroparisiphone.com/>
11. <http://senseable.mit.edu/eyestop/>

Bibliography

R. Ackoff, "From Data to Wisdom," *Journal of Applied Systems Analysis* 16:1 (1989) 3–9.

A. Adams and M. Sasse, "Privacy in Multimedia Communications: Protecting Users, Not Just Data," paper presented at People and Computers XV: Interactions without Frontiers, Joint Proceedings of HCI 2001 and IHM 2001 (Lille, France, 2001), 49–64.

G. Bell and P. Dourish, "Yesterday's Tomorrows: Notes on Ubiquitous Computing's Dominant Vision," *Personal and Ubiquitous Computing* 11:2 (2007) 133–143.

E. Ben-Joseph, H. Ishii, J. Underkoffler, B. Piper, and L. Yeung, "Urban Simulation and the Luminous Planning Table: Bridging the Gap between the Digital and the Tangible," *Journal of Planning Education and Research* 21:2 (2001) 196–203.

S. Benford, M. Flintham, A. Drozd, R. Anastasi, D. Rowland, N. Tandavanitj, M. Adams, J. Farr, A. Oldroyd, and J. Sutton, "Uncle Roy All Around You: Implicating the City in a Location-Based Performance," paper presented at the ACM SIGCHI International Conference on Advances in Computer Entertainment Technology (Singapore, 3–5, June, 2004).

C. Bettini, O. Brdiczka, K. Henricksen, J. Indulska, D. Nicklas, A. Ranganathan, and D. Riboni, "A Survey of Context Modelling and Reasoning Techniques," *Pervasive and Mobile Computing* 6:2 (2010) 161–180.

B. Biörnstad and C. Pautasso, "Let It Flow: Building Mashups with Data Processing Pipelines," paper presented at the Service-Oriented Computing – ICSOC 2007 Workshops (Vienna, Austria, 17 September 2007) 15–28.

M. Boyle and S. Greenberg, "The Language of Privacy: Learning from Video Media Space Analysis and Design," *ACM Transactions on Computer-Human Interaction* 12:2 (2005) 328–370.

O. Brdiczka, J. Crowley, and P. Reignier, "Learning Situation Models for Providing Context-Aware Services," paper presented at the 4th International Conference on Universal Access in Human-Computer Interaction (Beijing, China, July, 22–27, 2007), 23–32.

J. Burke, D. Estrin, M. Hansen, A. Parker, N. Ramanathan, S. Reddy, and M.B. Srivastava, "Participatory Sensing," paper presented at The World-Sensor-Web Workshop, 4th ACM Conference on Embedded Networked Sensor Systems (ACM SenSys) (Boulder, CO, 31 October–3 November, 2006).

F. Calabrese, K. Kloeckl, and C. Ratti, "WikiCity: Real-time Location-sensitive Tools for the City," in M. Foth, ed., *Handbook of Research on Urban Informatics: The Practice and Promise of the Real-Time City* (Hershey, PA: IGI Global, 2009), 390–413.

A. Campbell, S. Eisenman, N. Lane, E. Miluzzo, R. Peterson, H. Lu, X. Zheng, M. Musolesi, K. Fodor and G.-S. Ahn, "The Rise of People-Centric Sensing," *IEEE Internet Computing* 12:4 (2008) 12–21.

K. Cheverst, N. Davies, K. Mitchell, A. Friday, and C. Efstratiou, "Developing a Context-Aware Electronic Tourist Guide: Some Issues and Experiences," paper presented at Human Factors in Computing Systems (The Hague, The Netherlands, April, 1–6, 2000), 17–24.

J. Chin, V. Callaghan, and G. Clarke, "An End User Tool for Customising Personal Spaces in Ubiquitous Computing Environments," in J. Ma, H. Jin, L. Yang, and J. Tsai, eds., *Ubiquitous Intelligence and Computing. Lecture Notes in Computer Science Vol. 4159* (Berlin, Germany: Springer, 2006a), 1080–1089.

J. Chin, V. Callaghan, and G. Clarke, "An End-User Programming Paradigm for Pervasive Computing Applications," paper presented at the ACS/IEEE International Conference on Pervasive Services (Lyon, France, June, 26–29, 2006b), 325–328.

J. Corburn, *Street Science: Community Knowledge and Environmental Health Justice* (Cambridge: MIT Press, 2005).

C. Cornelius, A. Kapadia, D. Kotz, D. Peebles, M. Shin, and N. Triandopoulos, "Anonysense: Privacy-Aware People-Centric Sensing," paper presented at the 6th International Conference on Mobile Systems, Applications, and Services (Breckenridge, CO, June, 17–20, 2008), 211–224.

CUD, *Connected and Sustainable Mobility / Connected Urban Development* (2009), <http://www.connectedurbandevelopment.org/connected_and_sustainable_mobility/personal_travel_assistant> Accessed January 5, 2012.

D. Cuff, M. Hansen, and J. Kang, "Urban Sensing: Out of the Woods," *Communications of the ACM* 51:3 (2008) 24–33.

P. Dalsgaard and K. Halskov, "Designing Urban Media Façades: Cases and Challenges," paper presented at Human Factors in Computing Systems (Atlanta, GA, 10–15 April, 2010), 2277–2286.

E. Della Valle, S. Ceri, D. Barbieri, D. Braga, and A. Campi, "A First Step Towards Stream Reasoning," paper presented at the Future Internet Symposium (Vienna, Austria, September, 28–30, 2008), 72–81.

A. Dey, G. Abowd, and D. Salber, "A Conceptual Framework and a Toolkit for Supporting the Rapid Prototyping of Context-Aware Applications," *Human-Computer Interaction 16:* 2 (2001) 97–166.

J. Erenkrantz, M. Gorlick, G. Suryanarayana, and R. Taylor, "From Representations to Computations: The Evolution of Web Architecture," paper presented at the 6th Joint Meeting of the European Software Engineering Conference and the ACM SIGSOFT Symposium on the Foundations of Software Engineering (Dubrovnik, Croatia, September, 3–7, 2007), 255–264.

G. Fitzmaurice, H. Ishii, and W. Buxton, "Bricks: Laying the Foundations for Graspable User Interfaces," paper presented at Human Factors in Computing Systems (Denver, CO, 7–11 May, 1995), 442–449.

M. Foth, R. Schroeter, and I. Anastasiu, "Fixing the City One Photo at a Time: Mobile Logging of Maintenance Requests," paper presented at OZCHI (Canberra, Australia, 28 November–2 December 2011), 126–129.

R. Ganti, N. Pham, Y. Tsai, and T. Abdelzaher, "PoolView: Stream Privacy for Grassroots Participatory Sensing," paper presented at the 6th ACM Conference on Embedded Network Sensor Systems (Raleigh, NC, 5–7 November, 2008), 281–294.

R. Hague, P. Robinson, and A. Blackwell, "Towards Pervasive End-user Programming," paper presented at the Fifth International Conference on Ubiquitous Computing (Seattle, Washington, 12–15 October, 2003), 169–170.

K. Henricksen and J. Indulska, "Developing Context-Aware Pervasive Computing Applications: Models and Approach," *Pervasive and Mobile Computing* 2:1 (2006) 37–64.

K. Henricksen and R. Robinson, "A Survey of Middleware for Sensor Networks: State-of-the-Art and Future Directions," paper presented at the International Workshop on Middleware for Sensor Networks (Melbourne, Australia, November, 28, 2006).

J. Hightower, S. Consolvo, A. Lamarca, I. Smith, and J. Hughes, "Learning and Recognizing the Places We Go," paper presented at the 7th International Conference on Ubiquitous Computing (Tokyo, Japan, September, 11–14, 2005) 903.

S. Jordà, G. Geiger, M. Alonso, and M. Kaltenbrunner, "The reacTable: Exploring the Synergy between Live Music Performance and Tabletop Tangible Interfaces," paper presented at the 1st International Conference on Tangible and Embedded Interaction (Baton Rouge, Louisiana, 15–17 February 2007), 139–146.

C. Karat, J. Karat, and C. Brodie, "Why HCI Research in Privacy and Security is Critical Now," *International Journal of Human-Computer Studies* 63:1-2 (2005) 1–4.

D. Kim, J. Hightower, R. Govindan, and D. Estrin, "Discovering Semantically Meaningful Places from Pervasive RF-Beacons," paper presented at the 11th International Conference on Ubiquitous Computing (Orlando, Florida, September–3 October, 30, 2009), 21–30.

T. Kindberg, M. Chalmers, and E. Paulos, "Guest Editors' Introduction: Urban Computing," *IEEE Pervasive Computing* 6:3 (2007) 18–20.

V. Kulathumani, M. Sridharan, R. Ramnath, and A. Arora, "Weave: An Architecture for Tailoring Urban Sensing Applications across Multiple Sensor Fabrics," paper presented at the International Workshop on Mobile Devices and Urban Sensing (MODUS '08), (St Louis, Missouri, 21 April, 2008).

N. Lane, H. Lu, S. Eisenman, and A. Campbell, "Cooperative Techniques Supporting Sensor-Based People-Centric Inferencing," paper presented at the 6th International Conference on Pervasive Computing (Sydney, Australia, May 19–22 2008) 75–92.

D. Le-Phuoc and M. Hauswirth, "Linked Open Data in Sensor Data Mashups," paper presented at the 2nd International Workshop on Semantic Sensor Networks, (SSN '09), in conjunction with ISWC 2009 (Washington, DC, 26 October 2009).

M. Lee, Y. Uhm, Z. Hwang, Y. Kim, J. Jo, and S. Park, "A Ubiquitous Computing Network Framework for Assisting People in Urban Areas," paper presented at the 32nd IEEE Conference on Local Computer Networks (Dublin, Ireland, 15–18 October, 2007), 215–216.

E. Martinussen, J. Knutsen, and T. Arnall, "Bowl: Token-Based Media for Children," paper presented at Designing for User eXperiences (Chicago, IL, 5–7 November, 2007), 3–16.

McKinsey Co. Preparing for China's Urban Billion, (Beijing, China: McKinsey and Co, 2009), <http://www.mckinsey.com/Insights/MGI/Research/Urbanization/Preparing_for_urban_billion_in_China> Accessed January 5, 2012.

D. Merrill, J. Kalanithi, and P. Maes, "Siftables: Towards Sensor Network User Interfaces," paper presented at the 1st International Conference on Tangible and Embedded Interaction (TEI '07) (Baton Rouge, LA, 15–17 February, 2007), 75–78.

R. Murty, G. Mainland, I. Rose, A. Chowdhury, A. Gosain, and J. Bers, "CitySense: An Urban-Scale Wireless Sensor Network and Testbed," paper presented at the IEEE International Conference on Technologies for Homeland Security (Waltham, MA, 12–13 May, 2008), 583–588.

M. Newman, A. Elliott, and T. Smith, "Providing an Integrated User Experience of Networked Media, Devices, and Services through End-User Composition," paper presented at the 6th International Conference on Pervasive Computing (Sydney, Australia, 19-22 May, 2008), 213–227.

J. Nolan III, "Establishing the Statistical Relationship between Population Size and UCR Crime Rate," *Journal of Criminal Justice* 32:6 (2004) 547–555.

J. Paay, J. Kjeldskov, S. Howard, and B. Dave, "Out on the Town: A Socio-Physical Approach to the Design of a Context-Aware Urban Guide," *ACM Transactions on Computer-Human Interaction* 16:2 (2009) 1–34.

L. Palen and P. Dourish, "Unpacking 'Privacy' for a Networked World," paper presented at Human Factors in Computing Systems (Fort Lauderdale, FL, 5–10 April 2003) 519–523.

S. Patel, J. Rekimoto, and G. Abowd, "iCam: Precise at-a-Distance Interaction in the Physical Environment," paper presented at the 4th International Conference on Pervasive Computing (Dublin, Ireland, 7–10 May, 2006), 272–287.

E. Paulos, R. Honicky, and B. Hooker, "Citizen Science: Enabling Participatory Urbanism," in M. Foth, ed., *Handbook of Research on Urban Informatics: The Practice and Promise of the Real-Time City* (Hershey, PA: IGI Global, 2009), 414–436.

E. Paulos and T. Jenkins, "Urban Probes: Encountering Our Emerging Urban Atmospheres," paper presented at Human Factors in Computing Systems (Portland, OR, 2–7 April, 2005), 341–350.

P. Peltonen, E. Kurvinen, A. Salovaara, G. Jacucci, T. Ilmonen, J. Evans, A. Oulasvista, and P. Saasikko, "It's Mine, Don't Touch! Interactions at a Large Multi-Touch Display in a City Centre," paper presented at Human Factors in Computing Systems (Florence, Italy, 5–10 April, 2008), 1285–1294.

P. Peltonen, A. Salovaara, G. Jacucci, T. Ilmonen, C. Ardito, P. Saarikko, and V. Batra, "Extending Large-Scale Event Participation with User-Created Mobile Media on a Public Display," paper presented at the 6th International Conference on Mobile and Ubiquitous Multimedia Oulu (Finland, 12–14 December, 2007), 131–138.

B. Piper, C. Ratti, and H. Ishii, "Illuminating Clay: A 3-D Tangible Interface for Landscape Analysis," paper presented at Human Factors in Computing Systems (Minneapolis, MN, 20–25 April, 2002), 355–362.

H. Raffle, C. Vaucelle, R. Wang, and H. Ishii, "Jabberstamp: Embedding Sound and Voice in Traditional Drawings," paper presented at the 6th International Conference on Interaction Design and Children (Aalborg, Denmark, 6–8 June, 2007), 137–144.

J. Rowley, "The Wisdom Hierarchy: Representations of the DIKW Hierarchy," *Journal of Information Science* 33:2 (2007) 163–180.

S. Seitinger, D. Perry, and W. Mitchell, "Urban Pixels: Painting the City with Light," paper presented at Human Factors in Computing Systems (Boston, MA, 4–9 April, 2009), 839–848.

J. Shi, R. Zhang, Y. Liu, and Y. Zhang, "Prisense: Privacy-Preserving Data Aggregation in People-Centric Urban Sensing Systems," paper presented at the 29th IEEE Conference on Computer Communications (San Diego, CA, 15–19 March, 2010), 1–9.

J. Streefkerk, M. van Esch-Bussemakers, and M. Neerincx, "Field Evaluation of a Mobile Location-Based Notification System for Police Officers," paper presented at the 10th International Conference on Human Computer Interaction with Mobile Devices and Services (Amsterdam, The Netherlands, 2–5 September, 2008), 101–108.

A. Tibaijuka, Address at the 12th Session of the United Nations Conference on Trade and Development (UNCTAD XII) by Anna K. Tibaijuka, UN Under- Secretary-General and Executive Director, UN-HABITAT and Director-General, UN Office at Nairobi (UNON) (Accra, Ghana: UN-HABITAT, 20–25 April 2008) http://www.unhabitat.org/content.asp?cid=5684&catid=649&typeid=8> Accessed January 5, 2012.

K. Truong, E. Huang, and G. Abowd, "CAMP: A Magnetic Poetry Interface for End-User Programming of Capture Applications for the Home," paper presented atthe 6th International Conference on Ubiquitous Computing (Nottingham, UK, 7–10 September, 2004), 143–160.

B. Ullmer and H. Ishii, "mediaBlocks: Tangible Interfaces for Online Media," paper presented at Human Factors in Computing Systems (Pittsburgh, PA, 15–20 May, 1999), 31–32.

B. Ullmer and H. Ishii, "Emerging Frameworks for Tangible User Interfaces," *IBM Systems Journal* 39:3-4 (2000) 915–931.

UNDP and Human Development Report, (New York, NY: United Nations Development Programme, 2007/2008), 2007) <http://hdr.undp.org/en/media/HDR_20072008_EN_Complete.pdf> Accessed January 5, 2012.

J. Underkoffler and H. Ishii, "Urp: A Luminous-Tangible Workbench for Urban Planning and Design," paper presented at Human Factors in Computing Systems (Pittsburgh, PA, 15–20 May, 1999), 386–393.

J. Underwood, H. Smith, R. Luckin, and G. Fitzpatrick, "E-Science in the Classroom—Towards Viability," *Computers and Education* 50:2 (2008) 535–546.

M. Weiser, "The Computer for the 21st Century," *Scientific American* 265:3 (1991) 94–104.

K. Whitehouse, F. Zhao, and J. Liu, "Semantic Streams: A Framework for Composable Semantic Interpretation of Sensor Data," paper presented at the Third European Workshop on Wireless Sensor Networks (Zurich, Switzerland, 13–15 February, 2006), 5–20.

R. Wishart, K. Henricksen, and J. Indulska, "Context Obfuscation for Privacy via Ontological Descriptions," paper presented at the First International Workshop on Location- and Context-Awareness (Oberpfaffenhofen, Germany, 12–13 May, 2005), 339–353.

J. Wong and J. Hong, "Making Mashups with Marmite: Towards End-User Programming for the Web," paper presented at the Human Factors in Computing Systems (San Jose, CA, 28 April–3 May, 2007), 1435–1444.

F. Zambonelli, "Pervasive Urban Crowdsourcing: Visions and Challenges," paper presented at the IEEE International Conference on Pervasive Computing and Communications (Seattle, WA, 21–25 March, 2011), 578–583.

C. Zhou, D. Frankowski, P. Ludford, S. Shekhar, and L. Terveen, "Discovering Personally Meaningful Places: An Interactive Clustering Approach," *ACM Transactions on Information Systems* 25:3 (2007), Article 12, 1-31.

O. Zuckerman, T. Grotzer, and K. Leahy, "Flow Blocks as a Conceptual Bridge between Understanding the Structure and Behavior of a Complex Causal System," paper presented at the 7th International Conference on Learning Sciences (Bloomington, IN, July 2006), 27 June–1, 880–886.

Designing for the Situated and Public Visualization of Urban Data

Andrew Vande Moere and Dan Hill

Abstract *This paper investigates the concept of urban visualization, the visual representation of an urban environment through its intrinsic or related data, where its display is also situated within that physical environment. It describes how the principles behind public and urban displays can be combined with those of social visualization and persuasive computing in order to create discursive as well as pictorial representations that provide a better and potentially actionable understanding of urban issues to its inhabitants. We introduce the role of several related research fields, and analyze a set of representative case studies, taken from current best practice, academic research studies, and an experimental design studio course to highlight the typical issues involved in conceptualizing and implementing an urban visualization. Lastly, the paper proposes a set of design constraints that typically characterize an urban visualization, in order to guide the future design and evaluation of useful applications within the field.*

Introduction

Humans are becoming an "urban" species, living in a large number of vast urban agglomerations. In fact, more than half the people on earth now live in cities. By 2050, it is expected that more than two-thirds of the world population will (United Nations, 2007). Yet cities around the world face various challenges of which the changing demands of demographics, mobility, energy consumption, quality of life, crime dynamics, economics, resource use, waste, culture production, and consumption, are just a few. While most citizens are becoming increasingly aware of the environmental, societal, and economic challenges that surround modern urban living, only few might comprehend the driving principles behind these problems, let alone reflect upon how these affect the reality of their own daily lives. Anticipating, understanding, and reflecting upon such urban problems is complex because of the sheer quantity and variety of interrelated parameters that influence these phenomena and their inherent dependence on the local context and sensitivities of a given location. No two cities in the world, or even two neighborhoods within the same city, are identical in the issues that residents face. Solving urban problems now requires taking into account the cultural, environmental, legal, or societal reality surrounding a specific place, in which the subjective experience and opinions of citizens are becoming as important as the physical manifestation of buildings and public services in the urban landscape. However, more localized decision-making typically requires higher resolution information gathering, in terms of quantitative measurements of the environment, but also in terms of collecting qualitative feedback from the very people who actually have to co-exist with, and within, these data. In order to gain a truer understanding of the influencing principles and tendencies behind growing cities, one should consider how to make stakeholders—i.e., citizens—better aware of the true nature of urban challenges. By involving the local population in understanding the driving principles behind current urban issues, more widely adopted and competent actions such as those induced by legislation and policies will stand a greater chance of improving the quality of life in cities, especially when part of the solution requires city inhabitants to change their ways of living.

One of the most pressing issues in cities is how to make them more environmentally sustainable. We claim that in order for urban inhabitants to become aware and act towards a more qualitative and sustainable urban neighborhood, a new way of communicating information will be required, involving both discursive as well as pictorial representations. Therefore, in this paper, we present the first exploratory steps in investigating the potential of representing "urban" data, or data that has a contextual relationship to the immediate environment, within the public, physical environment of the city as a potential solution for conveying actionable knowledge to local inhabitants. Moreover, the compelling communication of relevant, localized, and situated information might even change the perception of the physical environment in which the display is located.

Economic and cultural activities such as heavy industry and physical trade once helped define the local character of a city and its people through the various perceivable traces of their physical presence, such as the smoke from factory chimneys, the noise of local food markets, the dynamic flow of workers walking back from the factories or docks, or commuters leaving their neighborhoods in the morning. As many "western" economies shifted towards globalized service- and knowledge-based work, such urban activities have now become largely invisible and homogenous, leaving little physical trace of production. If the character of a place is linked to its production, how is local character and culture generated when production becomes invisible? Leaving aside the possibility of rediscovering forms of production with more discernible outputs, we believe this lack of character is perhaps best countered through tracking the continuous generation of "urban" data, which potentially contains the traces of productive activities and the many unique characteristics of our built environment. Therefore, through applying the appropriate representative means, the identity of place could still be distinguished and highlighted, making the identity of a place more tangible and relevant. To convey the implications of this changing nature of a city, a neighborhood, or a street, we thus propose to look for it through the lens of urban data, in the form of real-time digital traces of urban activities, as well as their qualitative impact on the local environment. By sharing this information through an expressive and socially shared medium such as a public display, we expect a sense of responsibility toward a place could be reinstated, which might even have the potential of changing local habits, attitudes, or behaviors. In the language of urban planning and urban design, this might even become a new form of "place-making."

The City as a Locale of Data about and for Its Inhabitants

Since the appearance of signage in the pre-industrial city to support spatial orientation and way-finding, valuable and situated information has been continuously displayed within the urban environment. By exploiting digital advances in screen and networking technology, such representations now have the potential to reveal information that is relevant, timely, and engaging for city inhabitants. Several movements and academic fields are currently converging around the idea of public and situated visualization in the urban context. The following paragraphs provide a short overview.

Open Data

"Open Data" is a philosophy that encourages the free and transparent distribution of data without restrictions of copyright, governmental oversight, or other mechanisms of control. The open-data phenomenon has been motivated by social movements that favor openness and transparency and the recent push towards encouraging technology-enhanced forms of participatory and public governing. While this ideology is well established in the context of scientific research and the Web2.0 phenomenon, the open-data phenomenon is only recent in terms of public governance and the built environment. The cities of San Francisco (*datasf.org*) and London (*data.london.gov.uk*) have been some of the first official urban authorities that have opened up large datasets on, and about, the built environment under the umbrella of facilitating transparent, accountable governing and participative citizenship. However, releasing such data to the public can hardly be considered sufficient, since to be useful, these data need to be presented in easily accessible and understandable ways. In recent years, various citizen initiatives worldwide have exploited the right to access and reuse public information as strategic tools for political influence and social action. The graphical representation of such data has led to significant changes in legislation, and has encouraged debate, changes in public opinion, and true citizen participation. The shared co-analysis of common data by participants forms a critical part of participatory action research and design (Bødker et al., 1988; Ehn, 1990). However, for a participative tool of this nature to be successful, it should be designed in a way that fits into the existing communicative ecology of its "users," here the city inhabitants. For example, locally relevant information might be best positioned in places that residents pass everyday. We believe that citizens should be encouraged to become more aware of current urban challenges through understanding the meaning of the hidden data of a city, when they are physically present within that city. Such an opportunistic way of presenting information that is essentially situated in a local environment should more easily overcome the obvious motivational and accessibility issues that are faced by traditional media communication formats, including mass mailings, online websites, or smart phone applications.

Social Visualization

Visualization, the graphical representation of complex information, has already been used as a feedback tool in an urban context, such as communicating urban interventions to the public, or for facilitating forms of participatory design and planning. However, most such visualizations have focused on realistic or experiential simulations of potential outcomes, such as for conveying the immediate implications of climate change (Nicholson-Cole, 2005). Realistic visualization, however, tends to emphasize the visual aspects of change, which may exacerbate people's existing tendency to relate reality solely to what they can "see" in their own neighborhood. Unfortunately, most urban challenges are abstract in nature and relate to a wide combination of interrelated quantitative and qualitative factors.

Non-realistic visualization, or by its more appropriate term, information visualization, has the power to convey "invisible" data, which has no direct counterpart in physical reality. Such abstract data typically requires some form of translation or mapping through an explicit visual metaphor to be perceived and, potentially to be understood. Visualization of abstract information for citizens in not particularly new: social and cultural theories of everyday life have always been interested in rendering the invisible visible, and exposing the mundane (Galloway, 2004). This interest has created the field of "social visualization," which tends to focus on enriching social, electronic communication by making its rich and salient qualities visible in easily accessible and understandable ways (Donath et al., 1999). More recent developments in this direction have shifted towards democratizing the power of visualization and making its advanced features accessible and usable for the public at large. Accordingly, social visualization offers non-experts the chance to increase their understanding of complex information by the power of collective and collaborative efforts (Viégas et al., 2007). Moreover, recent research efforts in this direction have demonstrated how lay people can be encouraged to create public visualizations for communicative and participative purposes, which by itself provokes sufficient motivation to even spur significant social activities (Danis et al., 2008; Gilbert and Karahalios, 2009; Heer et al., 2008). A few recent projects have demonstrated how social visualization has the ability to engage people in socially relevant topics, such as "PathFinder," which allows citizen scientists to collaboratively discuss and analyze the data they collect (Luther et al., 2009), and "The Village Buzz," an electronic notice board system that collects, shares, and visualizes user-generated multimedia content surrounding an existing high-density urban community development (Button, 2008). In essence, there thus exist some early empirical indications that publicly available visualizations can become appropriate communication media for sharing, discussing, and co-producing socially relevant data.

Urban Computing

Recent advances in sensing devices, wireless network connectivity, and display hardware have made the ultimate vision of ubiquitous computing finally possible, in which the "computer" as we know it becomes embedded in the physical objects and surfaces of everyday life (Greenfield and Shepard, 2007; Mitchell, 2004; Weiser, 1991). Similarly, "urban computing" is the research field that aims to apply this technological integration into urban settings and lifestyles, including streets, squares, pubs, shops, public transport, public buildings, and any other space in the semi-public realms of our cities (Foth, 2009; Kindberg et al., 2007). Driven by the increasing availability of urban data, together with the rising affordability of environmental sensors and the now ubiquitous use of mobile communication devices, urban computing aims to instrument the human experience of public space with digital information.

While most current research in urban computing focuses on improving the efficiency and productivity of activities in the city by the provision of locative services (e.g., mapping, way-finding), there is a recent understanding that contemporary urban life consists of a much wider range of emotions and experiences that needs to be addressed (Paulos and Beckmann, 2006; Townsend, 2010). For instance, the public visualization of "urban" data can play an important role in providing a better understanding of a place, as it has already been shown that, by combining existing data repositories with real-time sensor measurements and qualitative citizen feedback, valuable alternative views of the city can be created, potentially even in real-time (Calabrese et al., 2007). Such representations typically aim to reveal the salient patterns of urban living or make the impact of urban activities and their regulation understandable, such as to produce original insights into the nature of the contemporary city (Read and Pinilla, 2006), to digitally model and simulate the city (McGrath, 2008), or to investigate the spatio-temporal actions and opinions of city inhabitants (Vaccari et al., 2009). However, the resulting visual representations of the city still tend to be presented on dedicated media such as websites or smartphone applications, which are conceptually as well as physically separated from the actual environment from which the data originates, thereby turning the urban experience into a virtual one.

Urban Screens and Media Architecture

Today's "urban displays" are publicly accessible interfaces that allow passers-by to observe and potentially interact with functional information, ranging from bus schedules to dedicated tourism information (Fatah gen. Schieck, 2005). Such electronic displays are becoming increasingly ubiquitous in our urban fabric, as they now appear in squares and parks, around public transport platforms and, more recently, on-board public transport itself (Fatah gen. Schieck et al., 2008). However, the ideas behind the urban screen are slowly entering the realm of architectural design and construction: architectural facades, which traditionally either embodied the style of a specific time period (e.g., baroque, modernist), or represented the public function of the building (e.g., bank, church) have reached the technological stage in which they can be constructed independently from structural building constraints. As the typical rigid, weight-bearing facade is transformed into a flexible, almost weightless skin, an increasing number of buildings are becoming augmented with digital media. Technically, the nature of such displays can reach well beyond the traditional flat LED screen and its derivatives and even become integrated within the actual architectural or urban design. These treatments can range from subtly integrated interventions within the existing environment, by, for example, augmenting street furniture (Gaver, 2002); to "architectural" information surfaces that exploit state-of-the-art developments in thermochromatic panels (van der Maas et al., 2009); to dramatic mechanical and inhabitable structures that are able to dynamically change their shape (Oosterhuis and Biloria, 2008).

Content-wise, the obtrusive nature of its typical large, light-emitting panels is turning "media architecture" into an expressive language in its own right, influencing our experience of public space (Venturi et al., 1977). However, the majority of currently existing media architecture installations serve mainly commercial, artistic, or entertainment purposes. As research in this field has been mainly driven by technical challenges such as the development of fast-responding lighting systems or kinetically moving structures, its potential impact within the social and urban context is still often overlooked. Yet, through its explicit public dimension, media architecture has the ability to reach beyond its functional aspects, which it has in common with other human sciences. Through its particular way of expressing values, media architecture has the potential to stimulate and influence the urban experience without necessarily presuming that, in and of itself, it will promote social development. By combining the concept of the urban screen with the visualization of situated and contextual information, media architecture can grow beyond the broadcasting of artistic visual imagery, public announcements, or persuasive slogans, as it could facilitate bringing about a new understanding of complex local issues.

Persuasive Technology

While placing electronic displays in a semi-public space brings about new opportunities in social, community-driven communication and collaboration, it also raises important questions about the actual social and interactive behaviors occurring around a shared, public screen (e.g., O'Hara et al., 2003), including the potential to shape the opinions, attitudes, and behaviors of its audience. Because of its unique qualities, an urban visualization has the theoretical ability to persuade, because it embodies the three functional roles of *persuasion* (Fogg, 2003): through sensing technology, a display can act as a tool that increases the capability to capture a behavior (e.g., measuring residential energy consumption, bicycle use, etc.); through its visual imagery, it can function as a medium that provides useful information, such as behavioral statistics or cause-and-effect relationships; and through its networking ability, it can become a social actor, encouraging community-based feedback and social interaction.

However, the use of modern sensing and display technology for persuasive purposes in an urban context seems still relatively unexplored and is still limited to two very specific types: commercial advertising, such as the use of interactive visual effects to attract the viewer's attention (Mubin et al., 2009); and normative communication, including the widely adopted real-time roadside speed meters (e.g., "Speed limit: 50/Your current speed is: 65"). Displays designed to persuade seem to focus on providing some immediate reaction to local actions. As demonstrated in online media, social networks can form a useful construct to support behavioral change that involves group dynamics and the sharing and emulating of values. While online social networks tend to track and highlight the sharing of virtual values, similar concepts can be imagined in the physical world: an electronic car speed road sign would then not provide a numerical car speed readout, but, might, for example, provide a rewarding experience only when a cumulative shared goal has been reached or contrast your car speed as a distant commuter with that of local residents.

Towards the Public and Situated Visualization of Urban Data

Visualizing complex information within everyday urban space is not a trivial task, as most city dwellers are well accustomed to ignore such public messaging, regardless of how large, brightly, or interactively the imagery might be presented. Accordingly, recent research on public displays and interfaces has been investigating the circumstances under which people actually "look" at such screens (as they tend not to) (Huang et al., 2009), how people can be enticed to interact with them (Brignull and Rogers, 2003), how the interest of people can be sustained beyond their initial excitement (Morrison and Salovaara, 2008), and how the interaction with public screens tends to change over time (Jurmu et al., 2009). While such studies reveal the driving influential factors behind the performance of such displays, few working prototypes have been designed that demonstrate the novel conceptual possibilities of visualizing information within an urban context. Therefore, the following sections provide a short overview of the current state of public visualization, seen through the lenses of three different practices: private and governmental conceptual proposals and real-world implementations, research through design studies, and educational design courses.

Best Practice: Current Concepts and Implementations of Urban Visualization

The U.S. Debt Clock (Wikipedia, 2011) located in New York is a continuously updated large-size dot-matrix display that presents an estimation of the current gross national debt in the United States, in addition to each family's share of that debt. (See Figure 1a.) Next to the immense size of the numerical values, the animated effect of the continuously increasing number is in itself a quite disconcerting way of alerting people of the relative speed of public debt acquisition. While its relevancy goes well beyond the immediate city neighborhood, its location in Manhattan, the financial center of the United States, is still quite apt. The display conveys a sense of urgency on a personal level, as the elusive total debt number is averaged to that of the level of a single, average family.

The Cykelbarometer (Mikael, 2009) in Copenhagen also displays numerical data, though with a more localized relevance, as it broadcasts the daily and yearly total number of bicyclists that rode past. (See Figure 1b.) Located at one of the main entrances of the city, the number counts upwards immediately after a bicycle is sensed, providing a sense of participation and belonging. The goal of this display is to inform as well as persuade onlookers to commute more with a bike: in fact, it is not about being the first, but about being the cyclist with the number 500,000, who will receive a free bike from the local city administration.

CityWall (Morrison et al., 2008), in contrast, is a more elaborate screen in the form of a multi-touch surface installed in the center of Helsinki, giving access to past and present events that took place in the city. Due to its advanced interactive features, it has been reported that passers-by seemed rather interested in the novelty and the playfulness of the interface, rather than the actual content.

(a)

(b)

Figures 1a and 1b: Examples of existing forms of urban visualization using digital display technology (a) U.S. Debt Clock in New York City and (b) Cykelbarometer in Copenhagen
Sources: (a) Wikipedia, 2011, (b) Mikael, 2009

Analogue versions of public visualization displays exist as well, as shown in Figures 2a, b, and c. The Tidy Street project (Bird and Rogers, 2011) consists of a huge historical line graph, painted with chalk on a common road, which reveals the historical electricity usage of the street's inhabitants, contrasted to the average values of other UK regions. Although the street display is temporary, it

Figures 2a, 2b, and 2c: Figures 2a, 2b, and 2c are examples of urban visualization using "analogue" display technology. (a) Tidy Street, Brighton (U.K.), (b) "Pollstream-Nuage Vert," Helsinki, and (c) "Big Vortex," Copenhagen

Sources: (a) Bird et al., 2011, (b) HeHe, 2008, and (c) realities united, 2011.

aims to motivate the local community to participate in lowering energy consumption and to support the display's continued upkeep. (See Figure 2a.)

Ars Electronica 2008 laureate "Pollstream—Nuage Vert" (HeHe, 2008) is a city-scale visualization of sorts, which transformed a cloud emanating from an electricity plant chimney into a meaningful projection surface: the more the local inhabitants saved energy, the larger the surface area that lit up through the use of a powerful (though low-energy) laser light. (See Figure 2b.)

"Big Vortex" (realities united, 2011) is a soon to-be-built built waste-to-energy plant that will represent a quarter ton of processed CO_2 emissions by regularly emitting a visible gas cloud in the shape of a circular smoke ring (or toroidal vortex shape). (See Figure 2c.)

In the project "Melbourne Smart City" (Arup, 2011), the global engineering firm Arup proposed several urban visualization concepts within the strategic framing of a smart city vision for the city of Melbourne. The proposed ideas ranged from relatively "traditional" large LED screens that reveal real-time, street-wide water and electricity use, to more futuristic public art installations such as a floating LED cloud that conveys patterns of urban activity as a form of shared artistic experience. (See Figures 3a and 3b.)

These examples, some already implemented, some still in a conceptual phase, demonstrate the relative infancy of urban visualization and the relatively limited data complexity (in terms of size and dimensionality) that has been exposed to inhabitants until now. It seems that the ideal vision of the so-called "real-time city" (Foth, 2009; Ishida, 2002), in which continuous urban data flows are commonplace and freely available, has yet to arrive. Instead, the data sources used in currently existing urban visualizations are still relatively "simple" in terms of their technical implementation, though nevertheless still hard to come by.

Academic Research: Investigating the Urban Visualization of Private Data

In our recent in-the-wild design study (Vande Moere et al., 2011), we installed a series of custom public displays on house facades in Sydney (Australia) to investigate the effectiveness of explicitly externalizing household energy consumption—information that is normally kept well hidden and private. During the 10-week study, the daily electricity usage statistics of several households were displayed on their respective houses, so that any positive or negative change in their habits became immediately comparable to those of other nearby households. As shown in Figures 4a and 4b, the study comprised a set of custom-designed chalkboards, which were hung on the facades of five different houses and on which the information was updated by hand by the researchers, once per day. The boards included several visualization techniques in order to investigate the specific factors that influence the effective perception of the information by inhabitants and passers-by.

We hypothesized that the public exposure of household energy statistics would have a positive and possibly a sustained effect on electricity use by triggering feelings of healthy competition, social comparison, or social pressure (Abrahamse et al., 2005). However, the effectiveness of the "public" context, in terms of explicitly comparing the behavior of multiple persons with each other, is still relatively contested: while some past studies showed immediate and positive effects (Brandon and Lewis, 1999, Egan, 1999), others have revealed how people

Figures 3a and 3b: Figures 3a and 3b are conceptual ideas of urban visualization for Melbourne's Smart City Program. (a) Civic Smart Meter: here streets and blocks broadcast their resource data (e.g., energy and water use), (b) The Net, a layered net of LED lights hangs over a Federation Square "laneway," displaying civic data in real time.
Sources: (a) and (b) Arup, 2011

tend to be concerned about the apparent validity of the comparison groups (Roberts et al., 2004). Public and open comparison of behavioral data has some important drawbacks: while bad-performing participants might change their behavior positively when being confronted with those of others, good-performing participants tend to do the opposite, as they feel much less encouraged when noticing their already positive behavior, and feel no immediate objection to move towards the "average" (Brandon et al., 1999).

The design through research methodology demonstrated some of the real-world challenges of urban visualization and the effectiveness of *in-situ* evaluation studies to measure the effectiveness of conceptually convincing ideas. For instance, while many real-time visualization techniques can be easily imagined, it becomes a challenge to design a publicly noticeable display that is cheap, sus-

(a)

(b)

Figures 4a and 4b: Design research on urban visualization. Comparative public visualizations of energy use statistics in Sydney (Australia). The boards showed a set of visualization techniques, including daily performances facts, a neighborhood ranking, an historical energy use graph, and a visual long-term reward in terms of a pictorial bar.
Source: (a) and (b) Vande Moere et al., 2011

tainable in itself, easily updatable, acceptable by local residents, but also resistant to the urban environment, including "real" aspects as materials, safety, vandalism, weather, council approval, privacy issues, and so on. This project also revealed some non-obvious motivational issues when urban data is put in the public realm, most of which are related to how people interpret "change" instead of absolute use values, our inept method of rewarding sustained behavior, and an inability to connect the insights derived from the visualizations into direct, positive actions. Accordingly, we believe more research is required on how to best present complex data in a public context, in terms of being understood as well as facilitating actionable sense-making.

Education: Design Studio Experimentation

"Urban Sensing" was a postgraduate design studio course organized within the Master of Interaction Design and Electronics Arts (M.IDEA) program at the University of Sydney (Vande Moere and Hill, 2009). Students were challenged to design and build a working prototype of an urban visualization within the existing context of a real-world urban location nearby the university campus.

The student design ideas were fine-tuned through iterative evaluation cycles of successive low- and high-fidelity prototypes on the intended site location, and by personally observing and reflecting on the reactions and opinions of actual passers-by. The course demonstrated the practical, real-world issues of designing a public and situated visualization, and the difficulties in inventing case scenarios that are both meaningful and feasible. The issues we encountered ranged from accessing interesting urban datasets that were actually publicly available (those that were, were taken offline after discovering our use), to confronting police officers worried about security who took down all our wireless sensor devices that were mounted on the site.

The following three student works, as shown in Figure 6, demonstrate the conceptual richness of "visualizing" urban data in more creative and artistic ways, unrestrained from council policies or pragmatic functional considerations. The "Lonely Traffic Light," designed by Silje Johansen, turned the inanimate and anonymous nature of an ubiquitous urban construct, a traffic light, upside down: an existing traffic light was electronically augmented to enable it to "interact" with its users, even appearing to express emotional responses to waiting pedestrians. Small proximity sensors recorded the requests from pedestrians to cross the street (i.e., when users pressed the green light request button), and the exact states of the traffic lights themselves (i.e., captured by a light sensor attached to the green pedestrian light). A rudimentary form of artificially intelligent personality was implemented through a rule-based behavior algorithm. The output mechanism of the traffic light consisted of text-to-speech messages that were emitted by a hidden, miniature speaker, as well as two real-time Twitter streams, one of which revealed the actual binary state of the traffic light, and the other its emotional response about the current situation (e.g., lonely, bored, stressed, all based on the sequence and time stamp of past events). The successful implementation proved the potential for augmenting existing urban furniture instead of developing dedicated displays, in particular as a way to exploit its explicit physical context (e.g., the combination of a waiting area, busy road, and a normally lifeless object) to encourage passers-by to contemplate the new situation. In the context of interaction design, a typical traffic light could be considered a relatively ideal "interaction interface," as it is equipped with one of the largest and most intuitive forms of input mechanisms (i.e., a big, shiny, metal button), while it is relatively easy to capture the full attention of multiple (and often bored) "users" during a relatively long period of time (at least when the light is red). Here, this interaction opportunity was exploited to orally inform pedestrians about their expected waiting time, which was calculated from past averaged measurements and the time since the light was last seen as green and to tell traffic-related jokes, whose duration depended on the expected waiting time. Occasionally, the traffic light communicated apparent emotional responses, such as utter irritation when people indifferently pressed the button numerous times. (See Figure 5a.)

Student Steven Lukman augmented a common traffic light with a more functional goal in mind: to inform the people approaching the traffic light as well as already waiting pedestrians about the expected waiting time for a green light. He implemented two wirelessly connected and "futuristic-looking" contraptions such that the approach and the waiting were transformed into a rather spectacular data-gathering experience. This was conjured via the sequential blinking of a series of red/green colored LED lights that denoted the passing of time, and a calmly rotating spiral of Perspex discs (causing a visual effect much like the rotating "waiting" icons found in operating system interfaces or on the façade of typical old barber-shops), all encapsulated in a protected transparent, vertical contraption. The two output devices were distanced from each other such that the interface attempted to convey the imminent change in traffic light state to oncoming pedestrians some distance away from the actual lights. While more subtle than the Lonely Traffic Light project, and undoubtedly more complex than necessary to communicate a waiting time, this project turned the everyday task of waiting into an aesthetic experience that rapidly became a popular conversation topic with passing strangers. (See Figure 5b.)

The "Urban Polling Device" by Jack Zhao, provides an alternative way to conduct and visualize opinion polls on public streets. The device enables pedestrians an opportunity to vote "for" or "against" a certain issue through physical interaction with a tangible device that registers their vote and displays the overall trend. Passers-by can rotate one of the two discs, which itself is accompanied by a tactile "click" and a sound to acknowledge the recording action. The middle circle contains a "=" sign, of which the separate physical parts can be electronically animated to resemble "> ," "=," or "<," depending on the acquired voting statistics. While the device has no direct interventions for obvious misuses like multiple voting, it still opens up the question of agency and cooperative behavior in urban contexts. It also hints at an urban experience that is increasingly "metered" through the use of sensors and other input devices, as well as a culture of participation and public consultation. As such, the polling device prototype suggests a myriad of potential applications in terms of gauging the responses of citizens via an opportunistic, everyday device in the street, and providing the results back to the people at large. (See Figure 5c.)

As an exploratory and research-led teaching course, we realize that much of the perceived innovation of the proposed student projects rests with the relative novelty of embedding alternative information displays in a real-world, urban context. Both the physical and social (Williams and Dourish, 2006) context plays a surprisingly important role in designing for urban computing: what might work fine in our design studio environment or a controlled laboratory environment, was often perceived completely differently on-site. The typical goal-oriented character of an urban dweller, together with the continuous stimulation of our human senses by attention-grabbing advertising, noisy traffic, the harsh

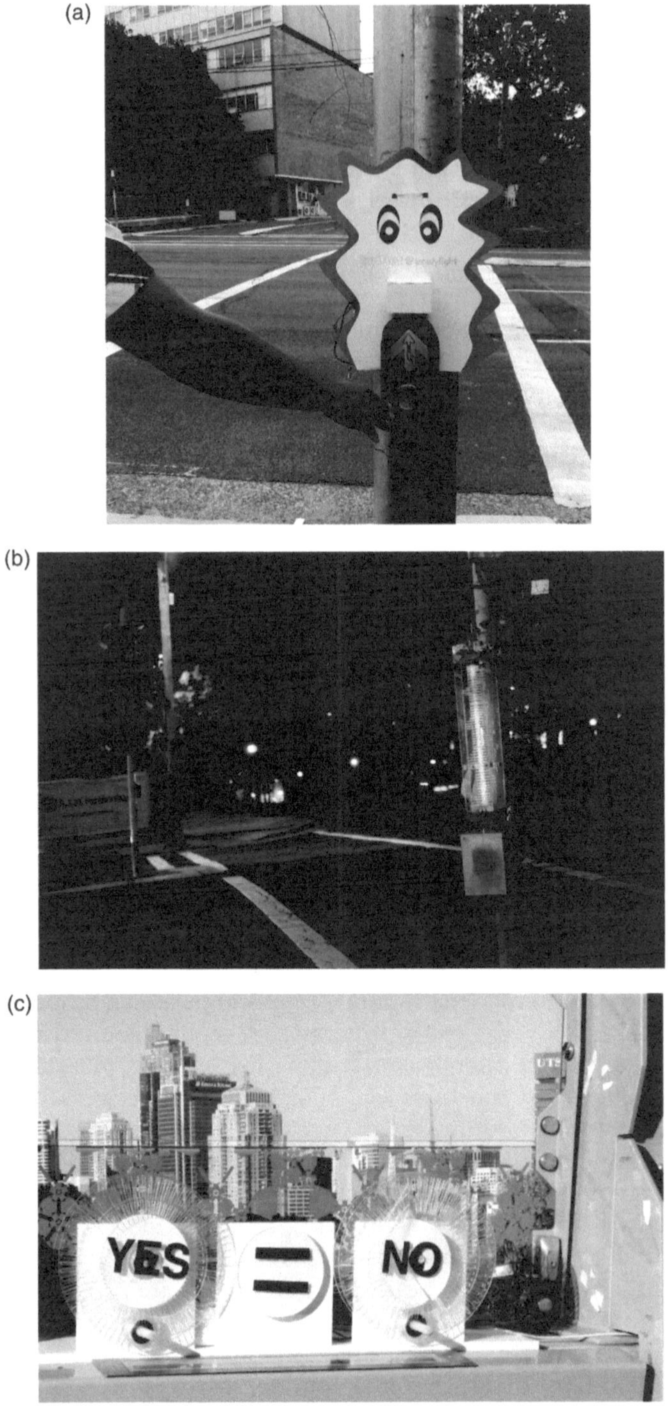

Figures 5a, 5b, and 5c: Figures 5a, 5b, and 5c are examples of design education in urban visualization. They picture experimental but working prototypes. (a) "Lonely Traffic Light" by Silje Johansen, (b) "Waiting Light" by Steve Lukman, and (c) "Urban Polling device" by Jack Zhao

Australian sun, and an amalgam of smells, makes the urban environment a particularly difficult context to design for. Accordingly, our students often did not anticipate how the vast majority of city dwellers would overlook their carefully crafted displays. Design subtlety and whimsy often had to be replaced with straightforward, large, robust, and "in-the-face" approaches that are difficult to ignore.

Conducting research through design outside of the typical lab environment proved to be a huge development challenge. As opposed to design interventions that tend to exist solely on paper or in virtual worlds, which all can be upgraded, downgraded, or tweaked at any time, the integration of "physical computing" in an urban context is often unforgivable in trivial issues, ranging from last-minute changes, however small, to common physical occurrences like a missing power source, an over-curious passer-by, a severe rain storm, or a nervous security guard. Although many user-friendly and open-source software frameworks have provided creative designers with the opportunity to step into technological territories normally reserved for the expert or hobby enthusiast, the key to successfully develop a convincing urban computing prototype seems to be mostly driven by thorough self-determination and the continuous urge to be critical of one's own work. Even the slightest technical error, caused by inexperience, trial-and-error, or just the occasional accident, will typically make an experiment fail completely, often even to a point where repair is too complex, time-consuming, or costly.

It should come as no surprise that some of the student projects, not shown here, failed to convince in terms of producing plausible, useful, and elegant urban design solutions that would genuinely enhance or contextualize the urban experience. As teachers, we could frequently employ a "so what?" test in order to gauge many of the proposed ideas, i.e. "So what if your system tells us the road is busy or the bus is just arriving; we can see that for ourselves..." or "So what if your data show a correlation between bike use and rainy weather; that is to be expected." Obvious reasons for the lack of surprising applications of urban visualization might include the high complexity of the design challenge itself, particularly for a largely foreign student cohort who had no personal experience with the urban context as a living environment, and, therefore, could not react to it as a design framework. In addition, the issue of providing city occupants with a "feedback" mechanism that transcended that of standard LED lights or LCD displays was often experienced as a creatively insurmountable bottleneck. The simplicity of programming blinking lights and housing them by rudimentary cabling was often too persuasive. In short, while these problems may reflect particularly on our students and/or us as teachers, still we get the sense that urban visualization itself could be caught between highly functional, almost banal components of urban infrastructure on the one hand, and highly abstract or oblique design interventions, interactive or not, on the other. This phenomenon may be a reflection of the open-endedness of the still emerging field at this time, partly because few of the more interesting datasets are actually available, or that the range of possible interventions into the urban experience is vast and effectively unconstrained.

Characteristics of an Urban Visualization

How is a situated urban visualization different from an interactive advertising billboard, an electronic council announcement screen, or a public, roadside speed meter? Based on the related fields and the examples that were discussed in the previous sections, we believe that its determinant design characteristics are threefold:

Situated

Here, "situated" means that the visualization is embedded in a real-world, physical environment.

Contextual. The visualization takes into account the unique characteristics of its physical location, in terms of both its explicit and implied meaning. An urban visualization often receives its meaning from the metaphorical context of its location, making detailed explanations unnecessary: a display attached to a house facade reflects the behavior of the resident household, smoke coming out of chimney represents pollution, a light-emitting artifact attached to a traffic light depicts a waiting time, and so on.

Local. The information shown has a direct and immediate relationship to the local context. This often means the data is sensed, measured, or acquired within the physical environment immediately surrounding the display, or has been modeled into values that reflect the particular circumstances of the people, buildings, or activities within the local environment. The data sets can originate from authorities, such as governmental or advocacy organizations (e.g., open data in the form of crime statistics, school inspection reports, etc.); crowd-sourced repositories containing geo-located information (e.g., Flickr, FourSquare), or from private or socially-motivated initiatives that employ their own environmental sensing devices (e.g., mobile phones, pollution sensors).

Social. The visualization reflects on issues that are closely relevant to the social-cultural reality in its vicinity. The local population can easily identify with the issues raised through the data, ensuring a level of usefulness and utility that goes beyond a specific time or a specific individual user (persona).

Informative

The data are different from those on posters and electronic announcement billboards in several ways.

Feedback. The visualization forms a direct feedback loop between the city, its inhabitants and their actions. Urban data are created by city inhabitants and are different from services, time schedules, or other urban phenomena that exist independent of urban inhabitants. An urban visualization thus forms a factual mirror, which must dynamically change according to the activities of inhabitants to be truly believable (and potentially persuasive). Equally, it may be that the form of the visualization itself needs to change over time, in order to retain the interest of its regular passers-by.

Insightful. The visualization allows onlookers to create meaningful insights beyond the retrieval of facts (e.g., events, routes, time schedules). Insights are discoveries of understanding that are essentially: complex, deep, qualitative, unexpected, and relevant (North, 2006). Allowing insights to be discovered has two main challenges: on one hand, the visualization should represent data phenomena (e.g., trends, outliers, clusters, contrasts) that are sufficiently complex and meaningful, on the other, the visual representation should be sufficiently intuitive to be comprehensible.

Consistent. The visualization in itself does not negate the meaning it conveys. Accordingly, a display showing CO_2 emissions needs to be sustainable in itself.

Functional

The following aspects assure the effective functioning of an urban visualization, which corresponds largely to the requirements of common urban displays, including advertisements, road signs, council announcement boards, graffiti, and so on.

Medium. The visualization is designed as to reach a sufficiently large audience, irrespective of their technical expertise, cultural background, or motivation. (Note: it may be that multi-sensory additions can successfully augment visualization.)

Participative. The visualization provides an experience that is shared by a community of people, potentially encouraging participative and collaborative action and the sharing of common norms and values.

Opportunistic. The visualization does not impede other urban activities. It is perceivable in the periphery of human attention, allowing viewers a free choice to dedicate their full focus or attention. Accordingly, its information is not of vital or crucial nature.

Aesthetic. The visualization is adapted to the urban fabric. It takes into account the constructive and aesthetic constraints of its surrounding environment and blends in visually as well as physically, and thus ensures a sustained acceptance by the local population.

Trustworthy. As with any public intervention, the visualization shows information in an objective, fair, and trustworthy way that accurately reflects the actual situation. For instance, the sources of the data that were used are clearly mentioned and are publicly accessible.

Persuasive. Similar to advertising and announcement boards, an urban visualization calls for some sort of reflection, change, or action. Designing and building public displays requires considerable time and effort, which typically must be compared to some sort of future benefits that offsets these investments. Or, put another way, the "value" of providing information to citizens centers around the general expectation that a more informed population tends to be more satisfied, more involved, leading to more informed discussion and participation in public discourse.

Following these design characteristics, it should be clear that an urban visualization should be ideally designed considering, or with the active participation of, the actual local citizens, in order to create a feeling of ownership and personal involvement. Notably, none of the characteristics defines the need for digital display technology: although the feedback loop between citizens and their activities through their digital data traces requires some form of dynamic updating, its display does not necessarily need to be updated in real-time. Similarly, the topic of interactivity has not been directly discussed. Interactivity should be considered more widely than the standard keyboards, multi-touch surfaces, or smart phone applications in order to guarantee a wide public acceptance, by those "users" who typically are not conscious of current technological advances.

Conclusion

The increasing presence of electronic communication devices in urban settings has the unfortunate tendency to reduce sociality. As a result, the role of the built environment as an ideal place for producing and sharing information is diminishing through the increasing interaction between computers and people. At the same time, developments in sensing, networking, and displaying technology have led to new forms of media that can be located in public spaces. Placing information media within an urban environment has the advantage of keeping the spatial experience tangible and multimodal, as opposed to the relatively one-sided and passive interactions with smart phones, even those that use augmented reality features.

The visualization of complex urban data on screens seems a promising technique to shape the next generation of public feedback. In particular, the insights from social visualization form a valuable platform on which applications can be built that have the ability to motivate and engage people in topics relating to urban challenges. Many current examples of urban visualization exist (see also Townsend, 2010), though most seem limited to the presentation of single data attributes (e.g., more or less energy consumption, total number of commuting bicyclists), that miss the opportunity to present more dimensional and rich relationships that form the very basis of the city as a complex system. What such visualizations should look like, where they should be located, and what issues they would be ideally suited to tackle, however, are some of the open questions that require further investigation, ideally through research on design methods. Viable examples might include feedback loops on living quality and satisfaction versus historical city investments, the impact of urban and legislative decision making, the effect of official traffic interventions on real-time traffic performance, the role of local inhabitants in creating a unique sense of place, and so on. Two of the fundamental prerequisites that would make this possible in the future are the opening of more public data with social interest and local relevancy, and an attitude change in tolerating citizen interventions in the public realm. Accordingly, not all of these applications can be commissioned, managed, or owned by city governments—indeed, an opportunity exists for non-governmental bodies to publish and manage such civic data, upon which others could build novel applications for, and hopefully with the full support of, local citizens. Once a sufficient amount of socially relevant and situated data become freely available, and local authorities have become more tolerant to bottom-up interventions within its, and our, public space, new kinds of urban applications will emerge that might even be able to compete with those that exist on today's mobile devices.

In the information society, it has become obvious that our cities are valuable and relevant sources of data that require rigorous aggregation, analysis, and public dissemination. This paper aimed to assess the still untapped opportunities of media channels other than the traditional computer and smartphone displays. We also argued that by returning urban data to citizens, those data can be used to create meaningful insights about the city and to become a form of knowledge that can lead to civic action.

Note on Contributors

Andrew Vande Moere is an associate professor at the Department of Architecture, Urbanism and Planning of the University of Leuven (Belgium). He is also the main author behind the weblog "Information Aesthetics" (http://infosthetics.com).

Dan Hill is at Strategic Design Lead, Sitra, Finland, and an adjunct professor in the Faculty of Design, Architecture & Building, UTS, Australia. While with Arup in Sydney, he worked on major urban development and building projects world-wide, from Helsinki to Masdar to Barangaroo.

Bibliography

W. Abrahamse, L. Steg, C. Vlek, and T. Rothengatter, "A Review of Intervention Studies Aimed at Household Energy Conservation," *Journal of Environmental Psychology* 25:3 (2005) 273–291.

Arup, *C40 Urban Life:* Melbourne Smart City (2011).

J. Bird and Y. Rogers, "The Pulse of Tidy Street: Measuring and Publicly Displaying Domestic Electricity Consumption," paper presented at Workshop on Energy Awareness and Conservation through Pervasive Applications sat the Eighth International Conference on Pervasive Computing (Helsinki, 2010).

S. Bødker, P. Ehn, J. Kammersgaard, M. Kyng, and Y. Sundblad, "A Utopian Experience," in G. Bjerknes *et al.*, eds., *Computers and Democracy: A Scandinavian Challenge* (Williston, VT: Avebury, 1988).

G. Brandon and A. Lewis, "Reducing Household Energy Consumption: A Qualitative and Quantitative Field Study," *Journal of Environmental Psychology* 19:1 (1999) 75–85.

H. Brignull and Y. Rogers, "Enticing People to Interact with Large Public Displays in Public Spaces," *INTERACT'03* (December 2003) 17–24.

A. Button, "Designing Social Tools for the Bees, the Buzz and the Beehive," *Australasian Conference on Computer-Human Interaction: Designing for Habitus and Habitat*, (ACM 2008), 323–326.

F. Calabrese, K. Kloeck, and C. Ratti, "Wikicity: Real-Time Urban Environments," *IEEE Pervasive Computing* 6:3 (2007) 52–53.

C.M. Danis, F. Viégas, M. Wattenberg, and J. Kriss, "Your Place or Mine? Visualization as a Community Component," *Conference on Human Factors in Computing Systems (CHI'08)*, (ACM 2008), 275–284.

J. Donath, K. Karahalios, and F. Viegas, "Visualizing Conversation," *Journal of Computer-Mediated Communication* 4:4 (June 1999).

C. Egan, *Graphical Displays and Comparative Energy Information: What Do People Understand and Prefer?*, Summer Study of the European Coucil for an Energy Efficient Economy (Mandelieu, France, 1999).

P. Ehn, *Work-Oriented Design of Computer Artifacts* (Amsterdam: Lawrence Erlbaum, 1990).

A. Fatah gen. Schieck, "Animate Space: Urban Environments as Medium of Communication," *Proceedings of the 5th Space Syntax Symposium*, Techne Press 2005, 1019–1031.

A. Fatah gen. Schieck, C. Briones, and C. Mottram, "The Urban Screen as a Socialising Platform: Exploring the Role of Place within the Urban Space," in F. Eckardt *et al.*, eds., *MEDIACITY: Situations, Practices and Encounters* (Frank & Timme GmbH, 2008).

B.J. Fogg, *Persuasive Technology – Using Computers to Change What We Think and Do* (San Francisco: Morgan Kaufmann, 2003).

M. Foth, *Handbook of Research on Urban Informatics: The Practice and Promise of the Real-Time City* (Hershey, PA: Information Science Reference, 2009).

A. Galloway, "Intimations of Everyday Life – Ubiquitous Computing and the City," *Cultural Studies* 18:2-3 (2004) 384–408.

B. Gaver, "Provocative Awareness," *Computer Supported Cooperative Work (CSCW)* 11:3–4 (2002) 475–493.

E. Gilbert and K. Karahalios, "Using Social Visualization to Motivate Social Production," *IEEE Transactions on Multimedia* 11:3 (2009) 413–421.

A. Greenfield and M. Shepard, *Situated Technologies Pamphlets 1: Urban Computing and its Discontents* (New York: The Architectural League of New York, 2007).

J. Heer, F. Ham, S. Carpendale, C. Weaver, and P. Isenberg, "Creation and Collaboration: Engaging New Audiences for Information Visualization," in A. Kerren, J.T. Stasko, J.D. Fekete, C. North, eds., *Information Visualization: Human-Centered Issues in Visual Representation, Interaction, and Evaluation 4950* (Berlin: Springer, 2008).

HeHe, "Nuage Vert" (2008) <www.nuagevert.org> Accessed September 1, 2012.

E.M. Huang, A. Koster, and J. Borchers, "Overcoming Assumptions and Uncovering Practices: When Does the Public Really Look at Public Displays? *International Conference on Pervasive Computing*, (Berlin: Springer 2009), 228–243.

T. Ishida, "Digital City Kyoto: Social Information Infrastructure for Everyday Life," *Communications of the ACM* 45:7 (2002) 76–81.

M. Jurmu, H. Kukka, T. Ojala, S. Hosio, T. Heikkinen, T. Lindén, and J. Riekki, "UBI-Pilot 2009: Longitudinal Living-Lab Deployment of aNetwork of Interactive Large Public Displays," *Street Computing Workshop, Co-Located with OZCHI'09* Melbourne, November 23–27, 2009.

T. Kindberg, M. Chalmers, and E. Paulos, "Guest Editors' Introduction: Urban Computing," *IEEE Pervasive Computing* 6:3 (2007) 18–20.

K. Luther, S. Counts, K.B. Stecher, A. Hoff, and P. Johns, "Pathfinder: An Online Collaboration Environment for Citizen Scientists," *Conference on Human Factors in Computing Systems (CHI'09)*, (ACM, 2009), 239–248.

B. McGrath, *Digital Modelling for Urban Design* (London: John Wiley and Sons, 2008).

Mikael, "Cykelbarometer – Bicyclists Count in Copenhagen" (2009) <http://www.copenhagenize.com/2009/05/bicyclists-count-in-copenhagen.html> Accessed September 1, 2012.

W.J. Mitchell, *Me++: The Cyborg Self and the Networked City* (Boston: MIT Press, 2004).

A. Morrison, G. Jacucci, and P. Peltonen, "CityWall: Limitations of a Multi-Touch Environment," *Public and Private Displays workshop (PPD 08)*(2008).

A. Morrison and A. Salovaara, "Sustaining Engagement at a Public Display," *Workshop on Public and Situated Displays to Support Communities. Co-located with OZCHI'08* (Cairns, Australia, December 8–12, 2008).

O. Mubin, T. Lashina, and E.v. Loenen, "How Not to Become a Buffoon in Front of a Shop Window: A Solution Allowing Natural Head Movement for Interaction with a Public Display," Proceedings *Conference on Human-Computer Interaction (Interact'09)* (Berlin: Springer, 2009), 250–263.

S.A. Nicholson-Cole, "Representing Climate Change Futures: A Critique on the Use of Images for Visual Communication," *Computers, Environment and Urban Systems* 29:3 (2005) 255–273.

C. North, "Toward Measuring Visualization Insight," *IEEE Computer Graphics* 26:3 (2006) 6–9.

K. O'Hara, M. Perry, E. Churchill, and D. Russell, *Public and Situated Displays: Social and Interactional Aspects of Shared Display Technologies* (Dordrecht, The Netherlands: Kluwer Academic Publishers, 2003).

K. Oosterhuis and N. Biloria, "Interactions with Proactive Architectural Spaces: The Muscle Projects," *Communications of the ACM* 51:6 (2008) 70–78.

E. Paulos and C. Beckmann, "Sashay: Designing for Wonderment," *Conference on Human Factors in Computing Systems (CHI'06)*, (ACM, 2006), 881–884.

S. Read and C. Pinilla, *Visualizing the Invisible: Towards an Urban Space* (Amsterdam: Techne Press, 2006).

realities united, "Big Vortex" (2011) <http://realities-united.de/#PROJECT,197,1?> Accessed September 1, 2012.

S. Roberts, H. Humphries, and V. Hyldon, *Consumer Preferences for Improving Energy Consumption Feedback*, Ofgem – Centre for Sustainable Energy, 2004.

A. Townsend, "The Future of Cities, Information and Inclusion" (2010) <http://iftf.me/public/SR-1352_Rockefeller_Map_reader.pdf> Accessed September 1, 2012.

United Nations, *World Urbanization Prospects: The 2007 Revision*, UDoEaSA-P Division, 2007.

A. Vaccari, F. Calabrese, B. Liu, and C. Ratti, "Towards the SocioScope: An Information System for the Study of Social Dynamics through Digital Traces," *Proceedings of SIGSPATIAL International Conference on Advances in Geographic Information Systems* (ACM, 2009), 52–61.

D. van der Maas, M. Meagher, C. Abegg, and J. Huang, "Thermochromic Information Surfaces: Interactive Visualization for Architectural Environments," *Proceedings of the Conference on Education and Research in Computer-Aided Architectural Design in Europe (eCAADe'09)* 2009).

A. Vande Moere and D. Hill, "Research through Design in the Context of Teaching Urban Computing," *Street Computing Workshop (co-located with OZCHI'09)* (Melbourne, Novermber 23–27, 2009).

A. Vande Moere, M. Tomitsch, M. Hoinkis, E. Trefz, S. Johansen, and A. Jones, "Comparative Feedback in the Street: Exposing Residential Energy Consumption on House Façades," *Conference on Human-Computer Interaction (INTERACT'11)* (Berlin: Springer, 2011), 470–488.

R. Venturi, D.S. Brown, and S. Izenour, *Learning from Las Vegas: The Forgotten Symbolism of Architectural Form* (Cambridge: MIT Press, 1977).

F. Viégas, M. Wattenberg, F. van Ham, J. Kriss, and M. McKeon, "Many Eyes: A Site for Visualization at Internet Scale," *IEEE Transactions on Visualization and Computer Graphics* 13:6 (2007) 1121–1128.

M. Weiser, "The Computer for the 21st Century," *Scientific American* 265:3 (1991) 94–104.

Wikipedia, "National Debt Clock" (2011) <http://en.wikipedia.org/wiki/National_Debt_Clock> Accessed September 1, 2012.

A. Williams and P. Dourish, "Imagining the City: The Cultural Dimensions of Urban Computing," *Computer* 39:9 (2006) 38–43.

Probing Streets and the Built Environment with Ambient and Community Sensing

Flora Dilys Salim

ABSTRACT *Data has become an important currency in today's world economy. Ephemeral and real-time data from Twitter, Facebook, Google, urban sensors, weather stations, and the Web contain hidden patterns of the city that are useful for informing architectural and urban design. However, often data required for informing a particular building or urban project is not available. In order to gather local and real-time data of the city, sensor devices, which are now embedded in today's urban infrastructures, buildings, vehicles, and mobile phones, have become useful tools for probing streets and the built environment. The proliferations of low-cost microcontrollers that leverage physical computing have also made sensor devices more accessible and easier to configure. The wealth of data from these sensors, if aggregated, synthesized, and analyzed, has the potential to increase our understanding of human and social behaviors in the city. This paper presents a number of projects which use ambient or community sensing to probe streets and the built environment in order to capture real-time and historical data that are pertinent to specific urban contexts. The data that was further analyzed could be used to better inform various stakeholders of the city in their decision-making processes, such as to assist travelers navigating the city by providing informed choices or to help architects or planners identify better design options in architectural or urban design, building retrofits, or new urban intervention projects.*

Introduction

Cities and communities are emergent and holistic living systems. Analyzing data flows from the urban environment is essential to reveal hidden patterns that can lead to understand the state of the city and inform new developments, building retrofit projects, or urban planning. For architects and urban designers, designing places and spaces begins with embodiment (McCullough, 2004), understood as an intrinsic yet emergent quality of interactions (Dourish, 2001; McCullough, 2004). In the current pervasive computing age, the boundaries between the physical and the digital have blurred (Salim et al., 2011), and the digital urban layer that embodies people and places has become as important as the physical layer of cities (Ratti and Berry, 2007; Santo et al., 2010). Place-based interaction can now occur naturally as users interact with places within urban spaces on both the physical and the digital layers (Salim et al., 2011). There are significant lessons and experiences that can be drawn from interacting with the local real-time data from a specific urban context, location, or space while formulating strategic and critical decisions over a site.

The first challenge is to identify the right data sources and gather the required data. To extract information, knowledge, and intelligence that can aid decision making, it is essential to analyze and synthesize data in its raw state. However, the dynamic spatio-temporal information about the city and how it is emerging over time may not necessarily be easily extracted from online data sources (Salim et al., 2010). Understanding the state of a city within a particular context, such as traffic congestion or public transportation, and a particular time period, is an arduous task. Real-time and historical data from the urban environment are large, complex, and may not be all relevant. Although there is already a great deal of processed data and increasingly available data in the public domain such as through Gov2.0 initiatives—attempts from government agencies to make government data more transparent and open and government's interactions with the public more participatory and collaborative (Mergel, 2010)—these data are in disaggregated forms and may not represent real-time situations. Collections of raw data from multiple sources and domains need to be "cleaned" in order that data aggregation and management can be applied. "Data cleaning" involves detecting, reviewing, and correcting inaccurate, corrupt, and incompatible data from datasets, archives or a database. A major part of any urban research involving non-standardized data sources is the process of "cleaning" the data. This pre-processing stage, before any data analysis can be performed, can be very costly and time consuming. In addition, often the data that we need when designing a particular building or urban site project is quite specific, such as the pedestrian volume and flow on a particular street during a specific time. Such data are unlikely to be available online due to the specific nature of the project.

When social, cultural, or behavioral data of a local site or community are not available, cultural probes (Gaver et al., 1999), which is a package of maps, postcards, and other materials useful in provoking inspirational responses, can be used as tools for gathering tacit or local knowledge. However, when traditional cultural probes are used to gather data, the responses are static and do not provide real-time and dynamic data that can show patterns of emergence over time. In order to investigate the flux and emergence of a particular urban context, new methodological approaches to gather and represent data are required. The ubiquity of personal and mobile computing, wearable devices, sensors, and digital artifacts in the built environment, which has transformed spatial interactions in urban areas as well as the way urban data are collected, holds the potential for a more efficient approach to gathering real-time and dynamic data.

This paper proposes the use of sensors as *urban probes* for investigating environmental, behavioral, cultural attributes of the urban environment in four case studies. *Urban probes* are functional artifacts that combine the technological and social aspects of urban computing to collect information about the users or the use of technology in real-world settings (Paulos and Jenkins, 2005). Paulos and Jenkins (2005) introduced urban probes that explore urban trash with elements of provocation to generate inspirational and playful responses. The urban probes that were demonstrated in Paulos and Jenkins (2005) were used for observing an urban public trash system and the response from the public or recipients of the probes for performing interventions and deriving the cultural meaning of a place.

In this paper, sensors will be used as urban probes, not just for investigating cultural meanings, but also for gathering information about the natural environment that may not require any human input or public response. The purpose of the probes, aside from being tools for information gathering, is for informing architectural and urban design projects and can be used as active urban intervention tools.

Ambient and Community Sensing with Urban Probes

The proliferation of sensors and Web 2.0 data contribute to new opportunities to extract emerging behavioral patterns of the city. Three types of existing urban sensors that can be used as probes are infrastructure sensors, vehicle sensors, and mobile devices. Ambient sensing, in this paper, refers to the use of sensors in the infrastructure, existing systems, or with do-it-yourself (DIY) urban probes. Community sensing requires public participation, employing mobile phones or physical computing prototypes, to crowdsource information when probing a specific issue. This definition extends Krause et al.'s (2008) definition of community sensing, which is a method to share and access data from privately held sensors such as mobile devices.

Archived and real-time data from sensors embedded in the urban environment provide the potential for monitoring the current operating conditions of a city. Lessons can be drawn from existing building projects that have good energy performance ratings, demonstrate sustainable building operations, or accommodate satisfied occupants. Solar and energy analysis can be performed on the existing land use of the built environment. Residential and office buildings are now installed with smart meters that stream real-time energy use data. Coupled archived socioeconomic data and data from energy simulations of the built environment, live sensor data after matching with expert domain-specific knowledge can provide information that is pertinent to discovering patterns of sustainable urban living.

Inherently, the issues of transportation are closely associated with urban living. Public transport and personal motor vehicles are major contributors to greenhouse gas emissions and air pollution in cities. Today's vehicles and on-road infrastructures are equipped with a large number of sophisticated sensory devices that are capable of monitoring and providing data pertaining to vehicle status, real-time traffic conditions, traffic incidents, and road crashes (Salim et al., 2008). Sensors, in intelligent transportation systems, are designed and created to monitor the conditions of the vehicles, the road, and the environment in specific vicinities, such as weather information and traffic conditions. Communication and satellite navigation devices are becoming intrinsic features of recently released vehicles. Global Positioning System (GPS) has been used widely in navigation, map creation, land surveying, and also in vehicle tracking.

Communities have also been probed using crowdsourced applications on their mobile phones. Urban commuters carry sensors embedded in their mobile devices. Mobile devices and smart phones are now equipped with GPS Accelerometers, compasses, and various other sensors. In addition, the rise of micro-blogging (Twitter), social networking (Facebook, Ning, Academia, and the like), and Web 2.0 powered with geo-tagging capabilities provide networks of emergence and convergence of spatial interactions and knowledge of and about our cities. With their mobile devices, urban commuters are able to tap into the online resources for tasks such as travel information, route planning, getting to the nearest points of interests, and much more. Mobile phone data can be mined to reveal hidden patterns, such as the project by Eagle et al. (2009) that employs mobile phone data to infer behavioral data of friendships.

Given the proliferation of open source microcontrollers, sensors, and actuators, new digital and electronic kits can now be designed and deployed as probes. This is particularly useful when existing sensor devices are not accessible or further customization is required. Open source electronic prototyping platform such as Arduino, which allows numerous types of sensors, actuators, and microcontrollers to be connected with household objects, computer codes, and digital devices, have popularized the "make" or do-it-yourself (DIY) culture (Hertz, 2011). The Arduino board with its family of sensors was chosen for several reasons; first was the cheap and ready availability of the device and its add-on components. Support for a wide variety of sensors, an easy-to-use development environment and a thriving open source Arduino community formed the other reasons. Arduino is open source, and it uses a variant of the Processing IDE and a modified version of C + + called Wiring as the embedded language.

Using the data gathered from ambient and community sensing as environmental or socio-cultural probes, these data are then further analyzed. When this information is used in the early stages of architectural or urban design, this will have a great impact on the project since 80 percent of design decisions affecting a building project's outcomes are made in the first 20 percent of the project life. If relevant public data exist from online data streams, social network data, or crowd-sourced mobile applications, the collected data need to be aggregated with the online data. This pool of data may then be analyzed quantitatively and qualitatively—and visualized. Quantitative approaches may include statistical and computational data mining. The domain experts need to interpret the results of data mining into knowledge that can be visualized, such as using mashup techniques. A mashup mixes information from various online data sources in order to present and visualize the data contextually to the user. A mashup represents contextual information for a situated purpose through "ingestion, augmentation, and presentation" of online information sources (Jhingran, 2006). This is useful for informing decision making processes in urban design or planning projects or performing interventions.

Using sensors as probes, individuals and communities can access and process digital data about their environment while interacting with that physical environment. Web 2.0 initiatives such as Open Street Map facilitate *"crowdsourced"* activities—public participation to contribute data and content to a specific application—in populating world maps. With the availability of Pachube, a site for publishing sensor data feeds, sensing with DIY urban probes has become collective and participatory. Hence, the use of such probes facilitates an integrated initiative of ambient and community sensing. A recent example of ambient and community sensing was the real-time radiation monitoring during the tsunami in Japan in March 2011 (Pachube, 2011). Using a Geiger counter to measure nuclear radiation, as the sensor of the probes, the data were streamed live to Pachube. A site was set up to mashup the geotagged sensor data with Google Maps to visualize the radiation across Japan. The real-time visualization showed a good indication where the radiation was the worst.

To probe the built or natural environment using ambient or community sensing, it is essential to establish the data requirements for the specific issue that requires probing and investigate the availability of sensors. If mobile devices are going to be used, special applications or "apps" may need to be developed for specific probing purposes. If data sources from existing sensors or the sensor devices are not available, then DIY urban probes need to be made using Arduino.

Case Studies

The following prototypes employ ambient or community sensing to probe the natural or built environment in Melbourne. An example of a DIY urban probe for environmental probing is *Ambient Light Informer*, a DIY urban probe for analyzing a site to inform the design of responsive louvers of a reading room in Melbourne Botanical Garden. *Automated POE* is a DIY urban probe that enabled the automation of the Post Occupancy Evaluation (POE) survey for probing occupants' perception of comfort in a particular building. *U&I Aware* is a project that uses infrastructure and in-vehicle sensors for probing street intersections. In two ongoing projects, *iCO₂mmunity* and *Transafe*, web and mobile applications were designed as cultural probes to gather data and improve our understanding of public perception of transport performance, sustainability, and safety. *Transafe* and *iCO₂mmunity* used mobile phones to probe streets and public transportation.

Ambient Light Informer

One examination of how urban sensing could work was a construct of a master level course in architecture offered at RMIT University in Australia. A student was given a design brief for a new reading space in the Melbourne Botanical Garden. (See Figure 1.) The reading space was to be designed to provide a good lighting environment for reading.

Figure 1: **(Left)** A site chosen for the pavilion in Melbourne Botanical Garden; **(Right)** The pavilion model

To inform the design, instead of using the traditional approach of using light simulation and a solar path diagram to predict the light level at different times of day, experiments were performed with a lux reader and *ambient light informer*, the DIY urban probe, made of a number of light sensors connected to an Arduino (See Figure 2) in the preliminary design processes. Although there can be a number of parameters in designing a comfortable reading space, such as noise, temperature, wind, and light, given the short time frame of the project, light was chosen as a design constraint of the reading space for proof of concept.

First, the student experimented with Rhino 3D models that are responsive to real-time ambient light data input from Arduino Light-Dependent-Resistors (LDR). Changes on the ambient light level trigger fluctuations on LDR readings, which subsequently trigger updates on the parametric models set in Rhino. (See Figure 2.) The parametric variations in the Rhino model are scripted using RhinoScript.

Second, the student visited a number of popular reading locations around Melbourne carrying the ambient light informer, which consisted of an Arduino light sensor and a lux reader to measure the ambient light level in these spaces. (See Figure 3.) After observing and analyzing these data, the student concluded that on average, Melbournians would find 580–600 lux a comfortable light level for reading. This particular part of the study was essential, given that there could be cultural differences in how people respond to light levels in doing specific tasks as well as regulatory differences in lighting requirements. This task was also performed to calibrate the Arduino light sensor.

Third, the student calibrated the reading of the Arduino LDR with the lux reader. (See Figure 4.) Given that the models set up in Rhino can respond to the ambient light level read by the LDR, the solution space for the optimal design can be narrowed to those that match the real-time ambient light data.

Finally, the student fabricated a number of pavilion models with different scales, colors (to simulate materials), and louver openings. (See Figure 5.) Within the fabricated models on site, he used an Arduino board and three LDRs to measure the ambient light level on site at different times to determine the best orientation, material properties, and angle of louver openings.

This experiment demonstrated the value of working with live/real-time ambient sensor data on site in the modeling process. It also demonstrated the use of embodied virtuality with physical models. The interaction with physical models became embodied since the meaning of the interaction took place at a certain time, in a certain location, and with certain constraints. The manipulation of placement, orientation, size, openings, shadings, and the timing of the experiments directly generated data streams that could have been further analyzed as

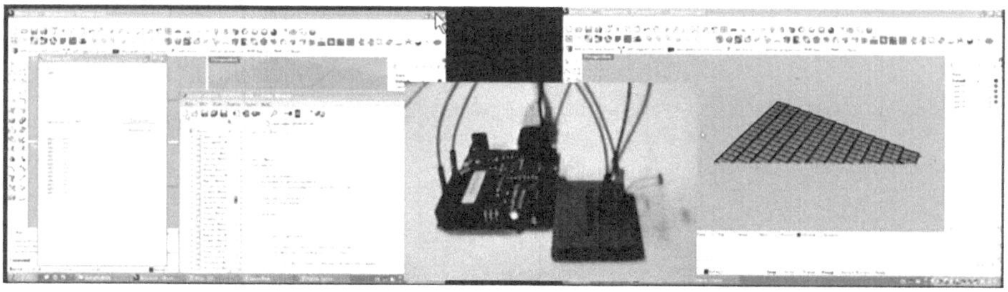

Figure 2: Responsive Rhino 3D models connected to light sensors

RMIT Building 8 Level 7(computer)		400-650 Lux
RMIT aisle		200-400 Lux
Swanston Library		400-800 Lux
RMIT cafeteria		200-400 Lux
Hungry Jack		550-600 Lux
Mel Central cafeteria Level 2		400-500 Lux
Mel Central aisle Level 2		200-900 Lux
Mel Central		1000-1300 Lux
State Library	(Public space)	300-400 Lux
		550-650 Lux
QV		300-900 Lux
McDonald		400-800 Lux
City Library	(Reading)	500-600 Lux
	(Multi-media)	300-550 Lux

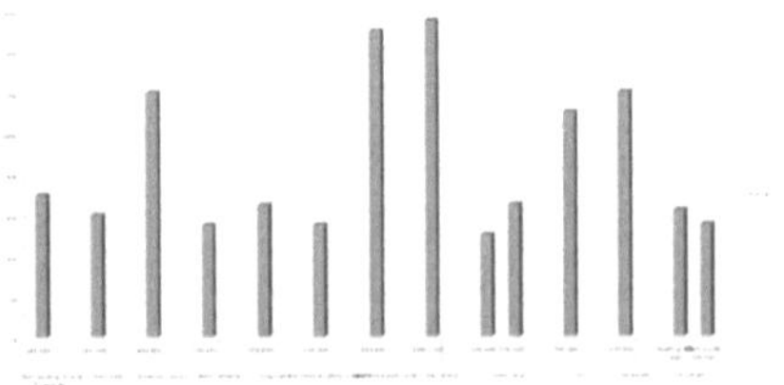

Figure 3: **(Left)** Popular reading locations around Melbourne CBD; **(Right)** The ambient light level measurement

input to the digital parametric models. Design decisions could be derived from the analysis of the ambient data that were streamed from the digital platform embodied in the physical models.

7:00	580	Lux	925
7:05	700	Lux	871
7:10	840	Lux	856
7:12	940	Lux	848
7:15	1100	Lux	832
7:20	1550	Lux	797
7:25	1750	Lux	784
7:30	2700	Lux	740

Light Reader:

580-600 Lux

For Arduino:

925~875

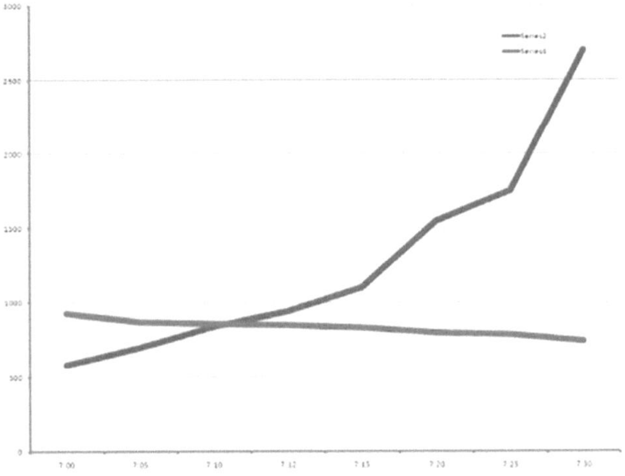

Figure 4: The calibration of the light sensor data and light reader

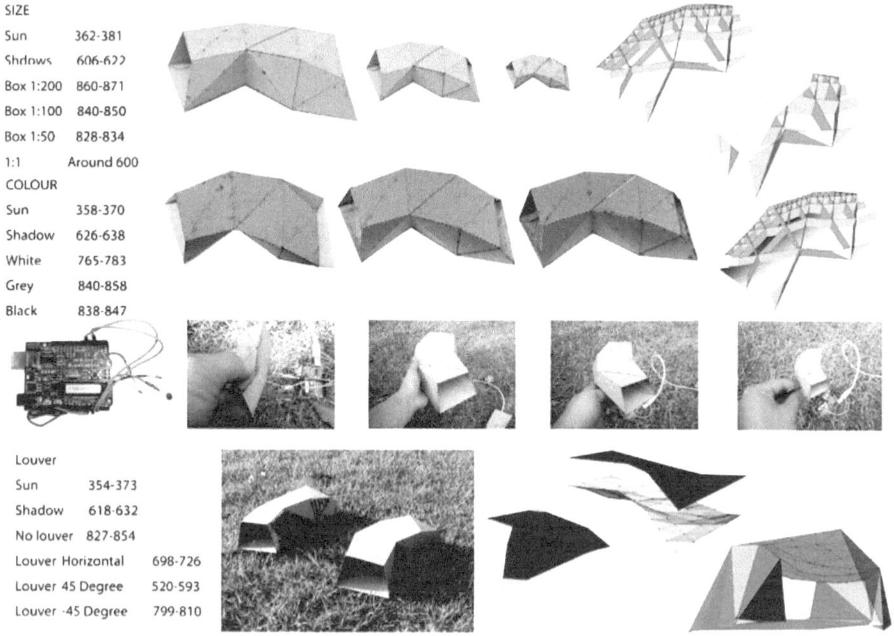

Figure 5: Ambient light analysis using Arduino and light sensors being placed inside the physical models

Automated POE

Architects and urban planners have long used design precedence and energy simulation for designing sustainable built environments. Simulation tools are used during the design stage to estimate projected energy use and carbon emission. However, the actual energy use measured during occupancy stage is often a lot higher than the estimated energy use in the design stage. In order to design buildings that yield high energy ratings and accommodate satisfied occupants, design precedence needs to be coupled with a comprehension of the ambient urban environment and an understanding of occupancy patterns.

The assessment of surveys on workplace conditions, termed as Post Occupancy Evaluation (POE), was conducted in the recently built office tower on the Monash University Caulfield campus, using a novel and non-traditional approach. This project was as a two-month summer project at Monash University.

POE study provides information that can be used either in modifying existing building systems or in subsequent building design to maximize productivity in the workplace by identifying previously successful combinations of variables under a building designer's control. These variables include, but are not limited to: temperature, noise, ambience, space, cleanliness, and lighting (Leaman, 2004). The POE surveys are usually paper based and completed by building occupants, since it is their comfort that the study seeks to evaluate. Naturally, this field is of interest to building managers.

It is possible for DIY probes to retrieve real-time ambient data and get responses from building occupants. The idea is to replace traditional paper-based POE surveys with a sensor powered system. A complete solution would be expected to handle most of the POE features (lighting, noise, etc.). In an experiment conducted at Monash University, Caulfield Campus by Prateek Rungta, a fourth year undergraduate Software Engineering student, a prototype was built around just the temperature variable. Besides a temperature sensor, it used a proximity sensor to detect movement around the device. The probe consisted of an Arduino circuit connected to a computer on which ran a controller program. The circuit components were the temperature sensor, the proximity sensor, and two buttons, each accompanied by a feedback LED.

The purpose of this setup was two-fold. First, it measured and reported the current indoor temperature. The controller program running on the computer would read, record, and report these temperatures. It would integrate these data with outdoor temperatures, that were obtained through the Web (via the Bureau of Meteorology). The second task performed by the circuit was the automation of the POE. The infrared proximity sensor would alert the circuit (and the controller) when someone approached the apparatus. The controller would then greet the person, report current indoor and outdoor conditions, and ask if the person was comfortable inside. The message played via the computer's audio output. The user could respond by pressing one of the two buttons (labeled "Yes" and "No") connected to the Arduino circuit. These responses would also be read and recorded by the controller. Thus the probes automated the survey for temperature related comfort. (See Figure 6.)

Each response was posted online on Twitter and on an RSS feed, using JSON protocol, to inform the building occupants. A Web mashup that compared the internal and external temperature of the building and the occupants' responses was registered. The data collected could be analyzed to extract information useful for POE and other stakeholders. It would allow observers to understand the patterns and perceptions of occupants' comfort. The early stage of the design of an urban public site may use similar installations around the built environments to gather public opinion for a crowdsourced POE from future users.

U & I Aware

Every minute, on average, no less than one person dies in a crash worldwide (Jones, 2002). The figure of the annual toll of human loss caused by intersection crashes has not significantly changed, regardless of improved road design and

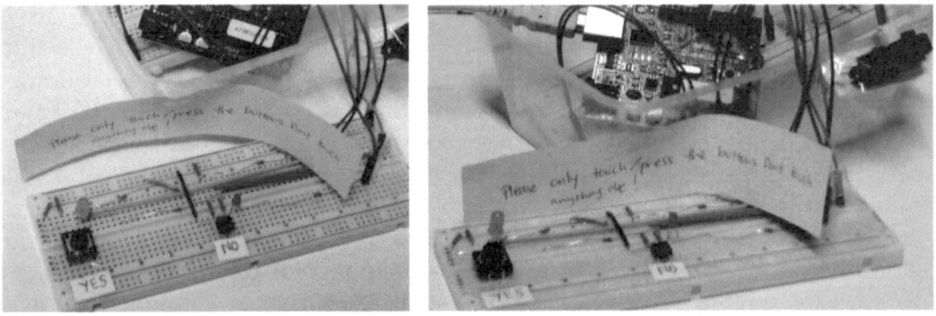

Figure 6: Automated POE physical tool

more sophisticated Intelligent Transportation Systems (ITS) technology over the years (US Department of Transportation, 2004). Human error is the major contributing factor to road safety risks. There can be various causes of human error, such as lack of situated awareness of the surrounding traffic, traffic blind spots, miscalculation of timing in performing certain maneuvers, or a deliberate violation of traffic regulations. This can be attributed to various road users with different cognitive and physical abilities/disabilities. Thus, behavioral changes need to be advocated through effective information delivery.

Each intersection is unique because of the diversity of intersections' characteristics such as different intersection shapes, the number of intersection legs, signalized/unsignalized, traffic volume, rural/urban setting, types of vehicles using the intersection, various average traffic speed, median width, road turn types, and the number of lanes (Salim et al., 2007a). Therefore, the complex nature of intersection collisions requires systems that warn drivers about the possibility of collisions. A meticulous study on a particular intersection by performing site study and observation is usually done to understand different issues in each intersection and perform intervention such as improving intersection safety.

As demonstrated in our previous work, the U&I Aware System (Salim et al., 2007b) is a context-aware framework for collision avoidance on road intersections. It encapsulates three components: collision learning, collision detection, and collision warning. The framework was designed as the basis for early collision warning devices for road users. In particular, the collision learning component employed existing in-vehicle sensors such as Global Positioning System (GPS) and forward, rear, and side collision sensor devices to analyze collision manoeuvers and near-collision events. Since these privately-owned probes were not available during the research, the sensor data were simulated. The collision learning component was equipped with data mining techniques to extract collision patterns from data streams from in-vehicle and on-the-road sensors. By analyzing the data from these sensors, we can derive collision patterns of each intersection which are then used to match driver behaviors with the knowledge base to predict future collisions. The collision warning system was simulated on mobile devices in each vehicle.

iCO_2mmunity

Public transport and personal motor vehicles are major contributors to greenhouse gas emissions and air pollution in cities. The City of Melbourne recently issued a publication that presented various strategies for reducing carbon emission 50 to 60 percent across the municipality by 2020 in various areas, of which passenger transport is identified as one of the key areas (City of Melbourne, 2008). In, 2003, 73.6 percent of total greenhouse emissions in Australia was composed of CO_2, of which 56 percent was contributed by electricity and heat production, while 15.9 percent was contributed by public transport and passenger cars (AGO, 2003; Coutts, 2007). The major causes of air pollution in the Australian urban context are motor vehicles (Australian State of the Environment Committee, 2001) as traffic contributes to 75 percent of the total urban air pollution (Simmonds and Keay, 1997). There is a need for a mechanism to quantify the impact made by individuals' choice on their travel modes and leverage the public awareness of the impact of their decision in a positive way.

The City of Melbourne (CBD and surrounding areas) receives 770,000 visitors daily (City of Melbourne, 2009). A major fraction of Melbourne's 770,000 daily visitors are commuters who live outside the city. The city's current residential population is around 90,000 (City of Melbourne, 2009). Melbourne increases its population by 1,700 new residents each week (Real Estate Institute of Victoria (REIV), 2009) and its population is predicted to grow by 1 million by 2030 (Department of Sustainability and Environment [DSE], 2002). The impending growth of the city will place more burdens on the existing transportation infrastructure and the road networks that are already heavily under-performing. This will affect specific urban issues, including road safety, carbon emissions, occupancy and comforts, and crime and safety.

Commuters' increasing travel-time will also increase the size of the personal carbon footprints of commuters. The increase of CO_2 is parallel to population and density increase (Coutts, 2007). In the City of Melbourne, the trends of atmospheric pollutants closely follow the trends of traffic volumes (Simmonds and Keay, 1997). Although railways accounted for only 2.5 percent of 2008 transport emissions, road transport accounted for 86.3 percent of 2008 transport emissions, an increase of 27.5 percent between 1990 and 2008. This is because 91 percent of the 770,000 daily commuters to the City of Melbourne work (City of Melbourne, 2009), opting to drive to work (IBM Press Room, 2010).

The clustering of population profiles, based on preferred transport mode, reveals trends that will be useful for government to formulate public policies for improvement of the system and public satisfaction (Salim et al., 2010). Since data for such a study is not available, we need to use an urban probe to gather a large dataset from the public, and Web and mobile applications are the best tools for this purpose. However, as previously discussed, to compel users to actively participate in the crowdsourcing activity through the application, there must be a value or benefit they receive from participating. Given the choices of various transportation modes in the city and different route options, commuters need access to an online advisory system that provides real-time information on the current and emerging conditions of urban transportation networks.

We propose an interactive and visual application that provides travelers and commuters with informed choices for commuting in Melbourne. iCO_2mmunity is an online application hosted on mobile devices and the Web, designed to provide commuters with comparison shopping and just-in-time informed choices for commuting in Melbourne. The interface provides users with personalized travel suggestions based on the priorities, schedules, constraints, location, and personal information of each commuter. (See Figure 7.) Users can personalize the application to suit their priorities and preferences in delivering informed choices.

Just-in-time informed choices are delivered based on profile and trip plans It has an intelligent feature that learns and senses individuals' transportation modes, quantifies their personal carbon footprints, and rewards those who choose greener commuting options. Individuals and organizations can also start green initiatives, such as offering car-pools or bike-share for commuting to work or school, and accumulate reward points. (See Figure 8.) The real-time information about the city and the transportation infrastructure is gathered from the crowd, sensors on the roads and public transports, and the Web. Users can submit their commuting experience and report the conditions of the road, bicycle track, footpath, stations, stops, public transport, wherever they are. The

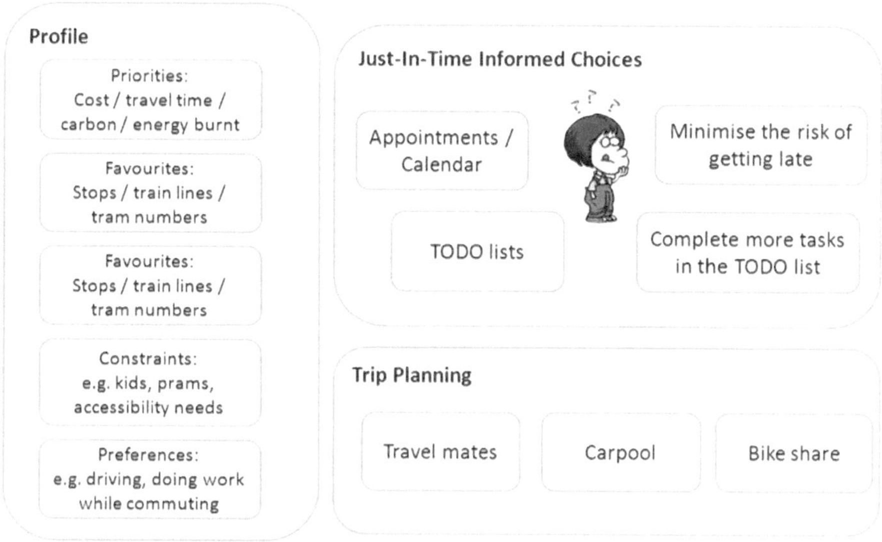

Figure 7: Just-in-time informed choices are delivered based on profile and trip plans

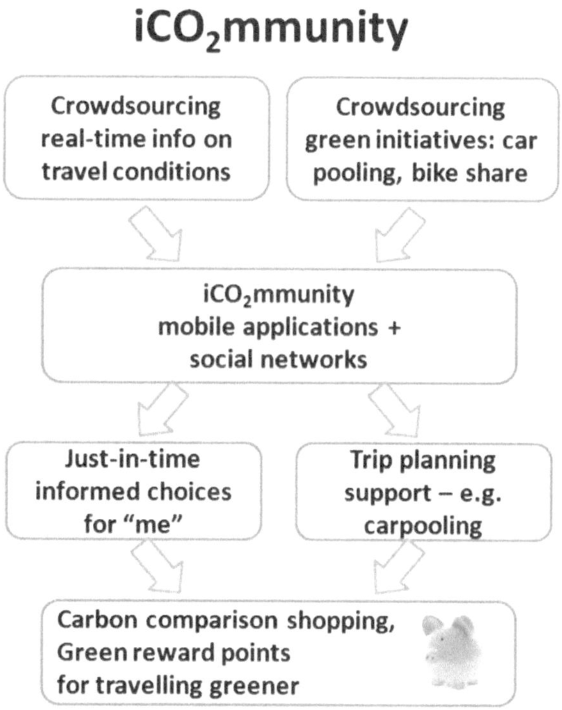

Figure 8: The data flow in iCO_2mmunity

result is a crowd-informed decision making support system for greener living and more efficient multimodal transport.

The persuasion for using the application comes from two key features, the first is the flexibility and usability of the application (See Figures 9 and 10),

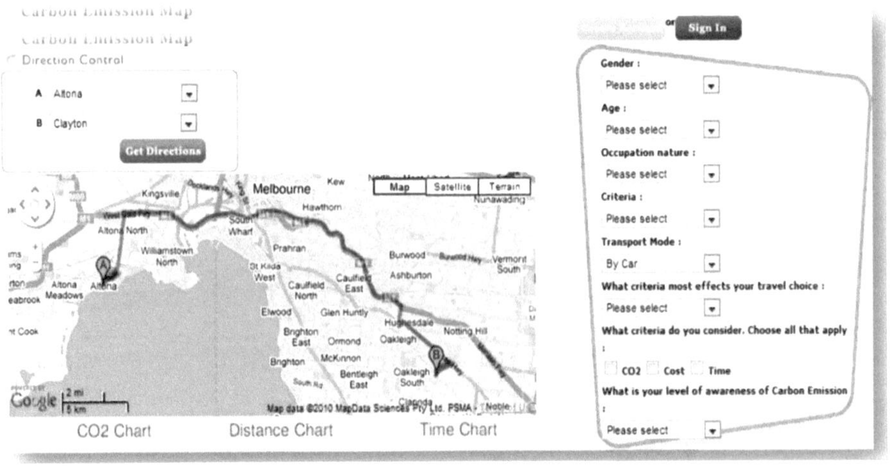

Figure 9: User input to the iCO_2mmunity web application

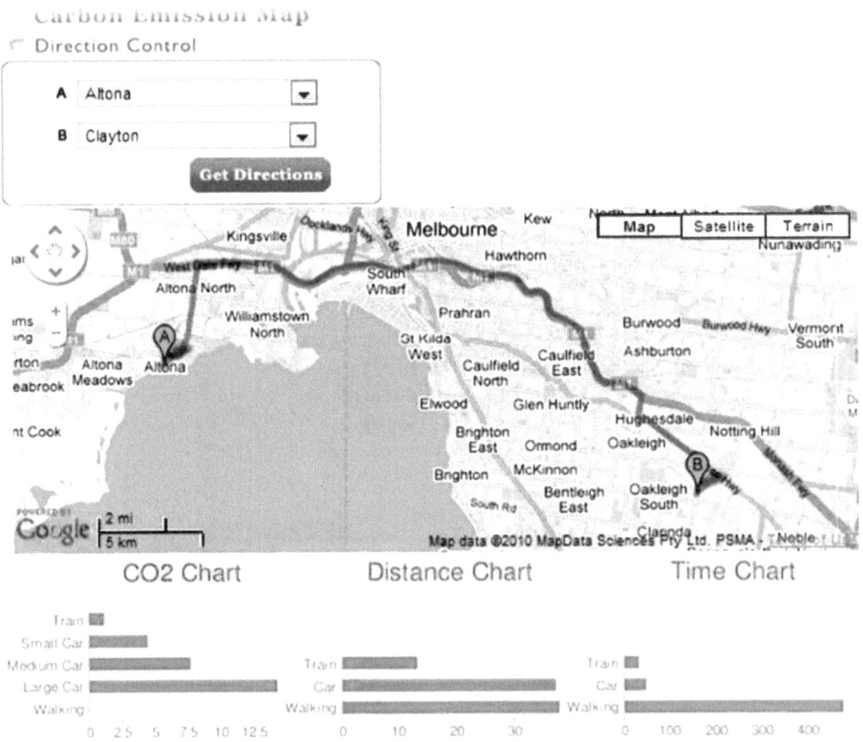

Figure 10: Three charts comparing CO_2, distance, and time

developed by Alhamazani (2010), to inform users based on their profile and preferences, and the second is the ability of getting green rewards for traveling greener. The rewards are termed as *carbon credit*, which can be used in a carbon trading system (See Figures 11 and 12) that simulates the idea of selling or

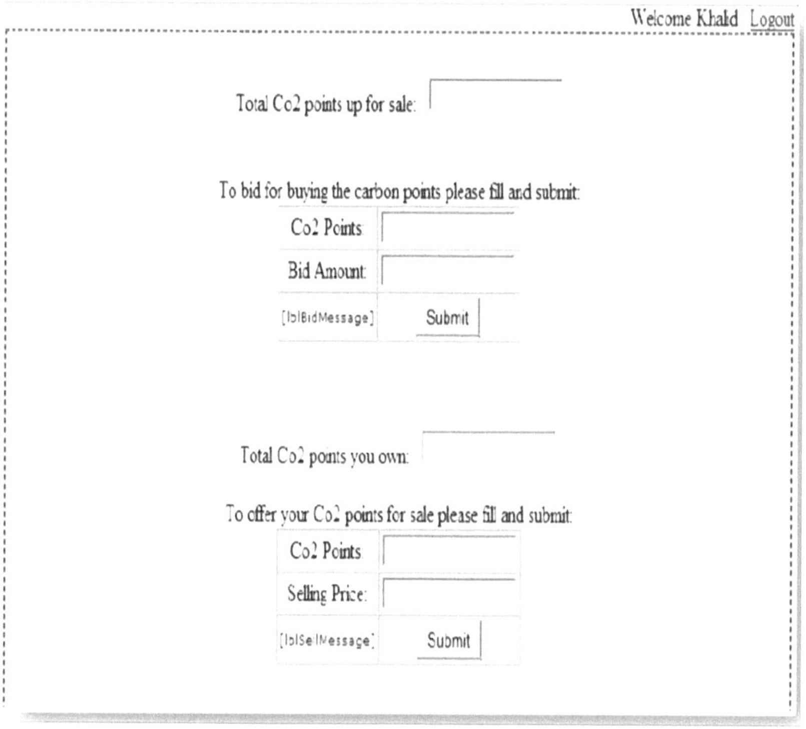

Figure 11: The main page of the carbon trading system

buying carbon points through a central system, also developed by Alhamazani (2010), based on the real-world Chicago Climate Exchange trading system (http://www.chicagoclimatex.com/).

With the need to increase Melbourne's livability amidst its growth, iCO_2-mmunity will help integrate live information sources and optimize multimodal transportation as a holistic system. Stakeholders and city planners will benefit from information about transportation use that is being crowdsourced in the system. The integration of live information will also increase the usability of information and awareness of greener, sooner, and safer journey planning for traveling across Melbourne. Such information, when analyzed and visualized in varying industry domains, can inform strategic decision making for the sustainable development of the city. Businesses and services in the city can benefit economically from a more manageable and streamlined transportation system. This project will also help prepare the community for carbon pricing, as there will be an increased awareness of each person's carbon footprint made during daily travel.

Transafe

Local media sources often report that a high percentage of commuters feel unsafe and vulnerable, particularly while traveling on public transportation networks (Herald Sun, 2010; The Age, June 9, 2010; The Age, June 12, 2010). In actuality, however, Melbourne has a very safe transport system and the level of crime occurring on Melbourne's transportation networks is dropping: in, 2005–06, 45 offences

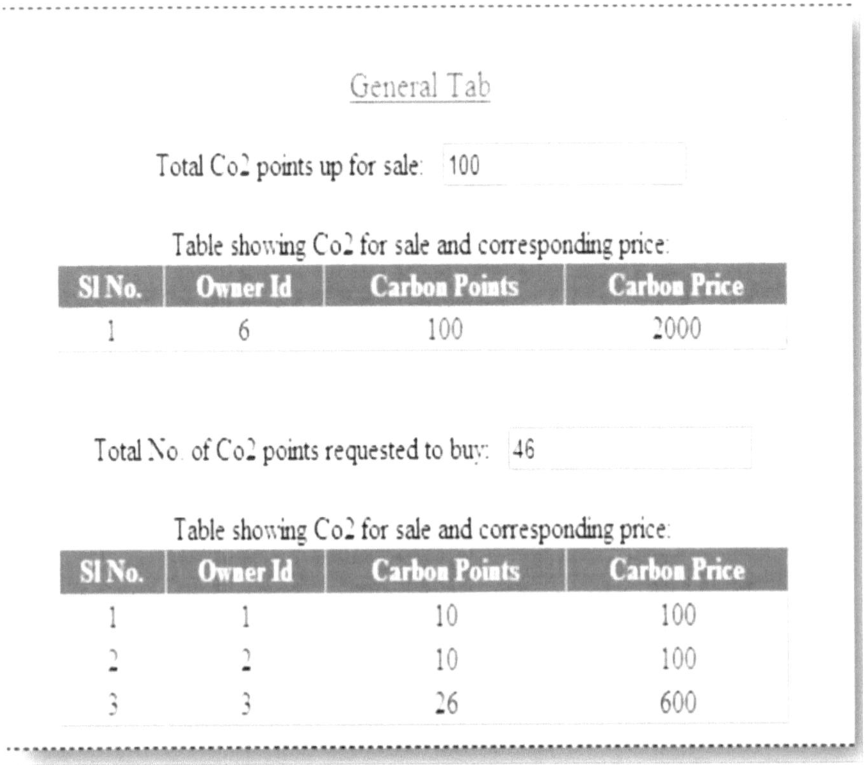

General Tab

Total Co2 points up for sale: 100

Table showing Co2 for sale and corresponding price:

Sl No.	Owner Id	Carbon Points	Carbon Price
1	6	100	2000

Total No. of Co2 points requested to buy: 46

Table showing Co2 for sale and corresponding price:

Sl No.	Owner Id	Carbon Points	Carbon Price
1	1	10	100
2	2	10	100
3	3	26	600

Figure 12: Transaction using carbon points

per million train passengers were reported, compared to 33 per million passengers in, 2008–09, where 75 percent of public transport offences in the City of Melbourne occur on trains, train stations, and station car parks (Victorian Auditor General, 2010). In contrast, the safety perception scores on Melbourne's trains is significantly lower than trams and buses, and has not improved over the last five years despite a statistical decrease in the number of offences occurring per passenger (Victorian Auditor General, 2010). The perception of safety is important as it influences how people feel about and behave towards their surroundings; however, perceptions of safety do not solely depend on levels of crime. Thus, the perception of high levels of crime on Melbourne's public transport can potentially introduce social barriers experienced by (tourist) visitors to Melbourne, international students, and locals who feel unsafe on public transport. Thus, understanding public perceptions of safety and developing policies and strategies to alleviate negative perceptions of crime and safety in the City of Melbourne have become key agendas of Melbourne City Council and Victorian State Government.

With all these complex sustainability, performance, and safety issues of public transportation, we need to gather public opinion and sentiments about Melbourne's transportation network. We use mobile devices as probes to crowdsource data from the public. The challenge of using mobile applications as probes to crowdsource information is that applications must be so useful, attractive, and persuasive that users will be compelled to actively contribute information. Fogg stated that a computer application can play the role as a persuasive social actor by rewarding the users with constructive feedback, simulating targeted user behavior, or giving social support (Fogg, 2002). The rapid advancement of Web 2.0 technologies has pushed the edge for online persuasion, given the ability of social marketers to "outreach" to larger online social players (Chinn and Artz, 2008).

When mobile phones are loaded with applications that enable crowdsourced content to be submitted, the applications would evolve over time with developers only needing to create an intuitive placeholder for the crowdsourced content. We call this *crowd place-making*, spatial movement of the crowd that is voluntarily reported via mobile applications that can track their locations using GPS and geo-tagging and accept rich user inputs about their whereabouts. Foursquare has become a popular social-networked, place-making application and has been used widely given that the app for Blackberry and iPhone are available and it is connected to Facebook's status updates. Users of Foursquare can "check-in" to places in the city, "shout" their status, and share tips about a place. If a place does not yet exist in the app, users can create a new place, add information about the place, and add it to existing categories (i.e. restaurant, entertainment, education, transportation infrastructure, shopping, and so on). This type of application is reliant on the crowd to populate the content and hence the existing application is capable of evolving from one use to another. Foursquare has also been used by shop and restaurant owners to promote their businesses by adding incentives and vouchers to those who are using Foursquare to "check-in" into their locations. Hence, the application has evolved from a purely place-making tool to a marketing tool. Facebook followed suit when Facebook Places was introduced.

Transafe combines interactive mobile applications with social media to capture and analyze public perceptions of safety to deliver "crowdsourced" collective intelligence about places in the City of Melbourne and their affective states at various times of the day (Hamilton et al., 2011). In contrast to a related precedent, Oakland Crimespotting, which is a project that mashes up crime data from local police authority and visualizes it in Google Map, Transafe gathers the locals' perception of crime and safety and compares it with data

Figure 13: Proposed Transafe platform

from local police and Crime Stoppers. Figure 13 illustrates the proposed platform for Transafe, centered around a mobile phone application that allows for:

- *Direct user interaction:* users interact with the application to submit and view crowdsourced crime and safety perception data. Mobile phone sensors will be used as input for user place-marking, timestamps, etc.
- *Stakeholder interaction:* organizations such as city councils, public transport entities, and state government can input infrastructure or (real-time) transport information and law enforcement can provide crime news and information;
- *User services:* improving personal safety perceptions through enabling a user tracking system, or connection to civil services such as emergency calls ('000') or criminal/suspicious activity reporting to Crime Stoppers.

As an urban probe, Transafe introduces the use of an "emometer," crowd voting mechanism with emoticons to encourage people to explain their feelings or perceptions of a particular place at any given time. These emoticons have ranges of intensity and so the user can provide an intricate color display of perceptions. A user can enter information about her perceptions of a particular area by selecting one or all of the eight emoticons with different colors representing

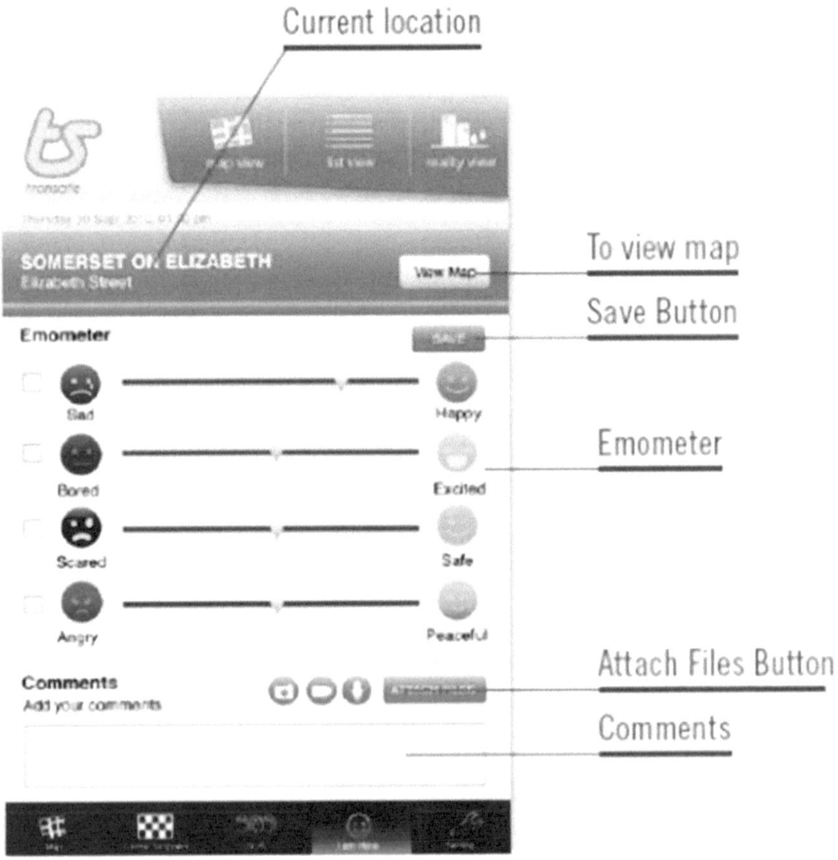

Figure 14: Emometer

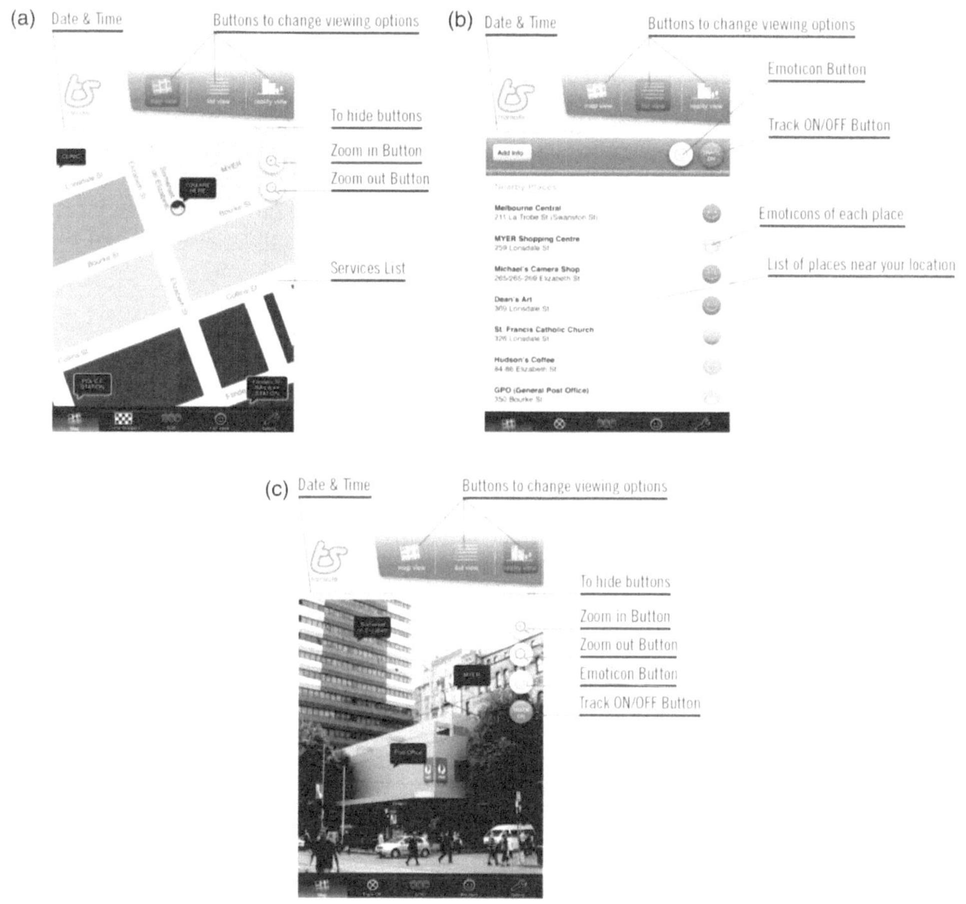

Figure 15: Multiple map view interface: (a) map view, (b) list view, (c) reality view

Sad/Happy, Bored/Excited, Scared/Safe, Angry/Peaceful sliding scales. (See Figure 14.)

The submitted Emometer data are then aggregated across the user crowd and the result will determine the overall color/mood of a particular area/locale. Visualizing the "feelings" of places in the city on different "map," "list," and "reality" viewing modes then allows for the user to see collective safety perceptions of places at different levels of granularity (See Figure 15): Figure 15a illustrates the "map" view augmented with the crowd's "mood" for each city block; Figure 15b shows the "list" view of the crowd's mood for particular buildings and landmarks; and Figure 15c depicts the "reality" map indicating nearby buildings and facilities.

Once the Transafe application has been fully developed, we will need to extensively test and evaluate it on a variety of users. We will need to enable recognition of the individual user contributions through the emoticons and the uploading of information. We need to explore the effective ways of influencing users to submit information to Transafe and hence build up the collective intelligence about the city. Transafe needs to be designed to encourage users to keep the application running and submit information to the Transafe crowdsourced database.

In the Transafe platform and mobile phone application presented in this paper, crowdsourced social network data can be clustered and labeled to discover patterns of public sentiments over a specific place in the City of Melbourne at different times of the day. Finding recurring patterns and monitoring emergence and changes of the sentiment patterns can inform us of specific activities, events, time, or places that affect public perception of safety. This, then, allows us to discover public perception trends in relation to various factors and user groups of the city. Such information can then be streamed back to the public or stakeholders of the city and better inform city planning.

Conclusion

We have proposed ambient and community sensing as a method for surveying the city for specific environmental, behavioral, and cultural investigations. Sensor devices can be used as urban probes to gather data that can be analyzed for urban intervention or informing design decisions in an urban project. The use of urban probes is instrumental for understanding a specific urban context. Types of urban probes include existing sensors embedded in the natural or built environment, in urban infrastructure and vehicles, mobile devices, and Do-It-Yourself (DIY) sensing devices. We have showcased five projects that employed ambient or community sensing prototypes as probes for a specific urban context. Future works include a tighter integration between ambient and community sensing by linking physical computing and mobile devices as probes and correlating data gathered from the integrated probes. The integration will provide a powerful combination of the extensibility, creativity, and customizability of DIY physical computing prototypes and the mobility, connectivity, and social aspects of mobile devices.

Note on Contributor

Flora Dilys Salim is a research fellow at the Spatial Information Architecture Laboratory (SIAL), RMIT University. She is also an Australian post-doctoral industry fellow in a project funded by the nationally competitive Australian Research Council Linkage grant to provide an integrated information system for multimodal public transport in Melbourne.

Bibliography

K.T. Alhamazani, *Pervasive Awareness and Persuasive Technology for Sustainable Travel Behaviour* (PhD thesis, Monash University, 2010).

Arduino <www.arduino.cc> Accessed February 24, 2012.

AGO (Australian Greenhouse Office), *Overview: 2003 Australian National Greenhouse Gas Inventory* (Canberra: Department of Environment and Heritage, 2003).

Australian State of the Environment Committee, *Australia State of the Environment 2001*, Independent Report to the Commonwealth Minister for the Environment and Heritage. (Canberra: CSIRO Publishing on behalf of the Department of the Environment and Heritage, 2001) <http://www.environment.gov.au/soe/2001/publications/report/pubs/soe2001.pdf> Accessed February 24, 2012.

City of Melbourne, *Zero Net Emissions by 2020 Update 2008* (Melbourne: Melbourne City Council, 2008) <http://www.melbourne.vic.gov.au/Environment/WhatCouncilisDoing/Documents/zero_net_emissions_2020.pdfAccessed> February 24, 2012.

City of Melbourne, *City of Melbourne Annual Report 2008–09* (Melbourne: Melbourne City Council, 2009) <http://www.melbourne.vic.gov.au/annualreport/ourcity_melbtoday.shtml> Accessed February 24, 2012.

S.J. Chinn and N. Artz, "Social Marketing, Social Networking," R.A. Oglesby and M.G. Adams, eds, *Business Research Yearbook: Global Business Perspectives* Vol. 15 (Beltsville, MD: International Academy of Business Disciplines, 2008) 395–400.

A.M. Coutts, J. Beringer, and N.J. Tapper, "Characteristics Influencing the Variability of Urban CO2 Fluxes in Melbourne, Australia," *Atmospheric Environment* 41 (2007) 51–62.

Department of Sustainability and the Environment, *Melbourne 2030: Planning for Sustainable Growth* <http://www.dpcd.vic.gov.au/__data/assets/pdf_file/0004/42772/2030_complete.pdf> Accessed August 21, 2012.

P. Dourish, *Where the Action Is: The Foundations of Embodied Interaction* (Cambridge: MIT Press, 2001).

N. Eagle, A. Pentland, and D. Lazer, "Inferring Social Network Structure using Mobile Phone Data," *Proceedings of the National Academy of Sciences (PNAS)*, 106:36 (2009) 15274–15278. http://reality.media.mit.edu/pdfs/Eagle_PNAS09.pdf.

B.J. Fogg, *Persuasive Technology: Using Computers to Change What We Think and Do (Interactive Technologies)* (San Francisco: Morgan Kauffman, 2002).

B. Gaver, T. Dunne, and E. Pacenti, "Design: Cultural Probes," *Interactions* 6:1 (1999) 21–29.

M. Hamilton, F. Salim, E. Cheng, and S.L. Choy, "Transafe: A Crowdsourced Mobile Platform for Crime and Safety Perception Management," paper presented at *ISTAS 2011: IEEE International Symposium on Technology and Society* (Chicago, 23–25 May 2011).

Herald Sun (2010), "Government Says Rail Crime Rate Dropping as Violence Hotspots Revealed," *Herald Sun* (June 28, 2010) <http://www.heraldsun.com.au/news/victoria/citys-most-dangerous-stations/story-e6frf7kx-1225884963316> Accessed February 24, 2012.

G. Hertz, "Arduino Microcontrollers and The Queen's Hamlet: Utilitarian and Hedonized DIY Practices in Contemporary Electronic Culture," *Proceedings of the 31st Conference of the Association for Computer Aided Design in Architecture (ACADIA 2011)*, (Banff, Canada, 11–16 October 2011), 44–47.

IBM Press Room, "IBM Global Commuter Pain Study reveals Melbourne Drivers Have One Of The Best Commutes In The World" (1 July 2010) <http://www-03.ibm.com/press/au/en/pressrelease/32029.wss> Accessed February 24, 2012.

A. Jhingran, "Enterprise Information Mashups: Integrating Information, Simply," *Proceedings of the 32nd International Conference on Very Large Data Bases*, (Seoul, Korea: VLDB Endowment, 2006), 3–4.

W.D. Jones, "Building Safer Cars," *IEEE Spectrum* 39 (2002) 82–85.

A. Krause, E. Horvitz, A. Kansal, and F. Zhao, "Toward Community Sensing," *Proceedings of the 7th International Conference on Information Processing in Sensor Networks* (St. Louis, MO, USA, April 22–24, 2008) 481–492.

A. Leaman, "Outside the Comfort Zone: Building Human and Basic Needs," *Human Gives Journal* 11:2 (2004).

M. McCullough, *Digital Ground: Architecture, Pervasive Computing, and Environmental Knowing* (Cambridge: MIT Press, 2004).

I. Mergel, "Gov 2.0 Revisited: Social Media Strategies in the Public Sector," *PA TIMES* 33:3 (Summer, 2010) 7, 10 <http://patimes.eznuz.com/printFriendlyPDF/articlePDF/22647.pdf> Accessed February 24, 2012.

Oakland Crimespotting <http://oakland.crimespotting.org> Accessed February 24, 2012.

Open Street Map <http://openstreetmap.org/>; Accessed February 24, 2012.

Pachube, "Crowdsourced Real-Time Radiation Monitoring in Japan" (March 24, 2011), pachube.com <http://community.pachube.com/node/611#3d> Accessed February 24, 2012.

E. Paulos and T. Jenkins, "Urban Probes: Encountering Our Emerging Urban Atmospheres," *Proceedings of the SIGCHI Conference on Human Factors in Computing Systems (CHI)* 2005).

C. Ratti and D. Berry, "Sense of the City: Wireless and the Emergence of Real-time Urban Systems," in V. Chatelet, ed, *Interactive Cities* (Orleans: Editions HYX, 2007).

Real Estate Institute of Victoria (REIV), *REIV Submission to the Outer Suburban/Interface Services and Development Committee Inquiry into the Impact of the State Government's Decision to Change the Urban Growth Boundary* (2009) <http://www.parliament.vic.gov.au/images/stories/committees/osisdv/iugb/OSISDC_UGB_sub90_REIV_12.10.09.pdf> Accessed August 12, 2012.

F.D. Salim, S.W. Loke, A. Rakotonirainy, B. Srinivasan, and S. Krishnaswamy, "Collision Pattern Modelling and Real-Time Collision Detection at Road Intersections," *Proceedings of the 2007 IEEE Intelligent Transportation Systems Conference* (Seattle, USA, 30 September–3 October, 2007a), (pp. 161–166).

F.D. Salim, S.W. Loke, A. Rakotonirainy, B. Srinivasan, and S. Krishnaswamy, "U&I Aware: A Framework Using Data Mining and Collision Detection to Increase Awareness for Intersection Users," *The 21st International Conference on Advanced Information Networking and Applications Workshops* (Niagara Falls, Canada, 21–23 May 2007b) 530–535.

F.D. Salim, L. Cai, M. Indrawan, and S.W. Loke, "Road Intersections as Pervasive Computing Environments: Towards a Multiagent Real-Time Collision Warning System," *Proceedings of the Sixth Annual IEEE International Conference on Pervasive Computing and Communications (PerCom 2008)* (US: IEEE, 2008) 621–626.

F.D. Salim, J. Burry, D. Taniar, V.C. Lee, and A. Burrow, "The Digital Emerging and Converging Bits of Urbanism," *Proceedings of eCAADe 28th Conference: Future Cities* (Zurich, Switzerland, 15–18 September 2010) 883–891.

F.D. Salim, H. Mulder, and J. Burry, "Form Fostering: A Novel Design Approach for Interacting with Parametric Models in the Embodied Virtuality," *Journal of Information Technology in Construction (ITcon)* 16 (2011) 135–150.

Y. Santo, J.H. Frazer, and R. Drogemuller, "Co-adaptive Environments: Investigation into Computer and Network Enhanced Adaptable, Sustainable and Participatory Environments," *Proceedings of eCAADe 28th Conference: Future Cities* (Zurich, Switzerland, 15–18 September 2010) 677–686.

I. Simmonds and K. Keay, "Weekly Cycle of Meteorological Variations in Melbourne and the Role of Pollution and Anthropogenic Heat Release," *Atmospheric Environment* 31 (1997) 1589–1603.

The Age, "Tram Violence Taskforce Dissolved," *The Age* (June 9, 2010) <http://www.theage.com.au/victoria/tram-violence-taskforce-dissolved-20100608-xtog.html> Accessed February 24, 2012.

The Age, "'It's a war zone,' Say Melbourne's Train Drivers," *The Age* (June 12, 2010) <http://www.theage.com.au/victoria/its-a-war-zone-say-melbournes-train-drivers-20100611-y3o7.html> Accessed February 24, 2012.

US Department of Transportation—Federal Highway Administration and Institute of Transportation Engineers, *Intersection Safety Briefing Sheet* (2004), <http://www.ite.org/decade/pubs/BriefingSheets.pdf> Accessed February 24, 2012.

Victorian Auditor General, "Victorian Auditor General's Report: Personal Safety and Security on the Metropolitan Train System" (Victorian Auditor General's Report, June 2010) <http://download.audit.vic.gov.au/files/20100609_Rail_Safety_Full_Report.pdf> Accessed February 24, 2012.

User-Led Design in the Urban/Domestic Environment

Georgina Voss and Natasha Carolan

Abstract *Urban spaces are pervaded by interpretive and reactive technologies that shape and are shaped by its inhabitants, with an increasingly active role for citizen technologists. Yet the role of domestic spaces in shaping lived experience within the urban environment, and subsequent technological interventions, is often overlooked. Homes are framed as closed-off environments which isolate their inhabitants from the city, despite being porous spaces that are also filled with ubiquitous computing. In this paper we draw on the participatory design and user innovation literatures to present the methodology for the "Homesense" research project that explored how users design and develop "smart" technologies within their own homes, based on the intersection of their concurrent urban/domestic lived experience. Kits of open-source hardware were used as cultural probes, and co-located "lead users" provided technical expertise. This methodology demonstrates the importance of physical space and location in user-led domestic activities, and of combinations of technical and "lived" expertise in developing these interventions.*

Introduction

The city is saturated in technology. As sites of the collective semi-public activity of impermanent, selective and itinerant inhabitants, urban environments are increasingly pervaded by technologies that shape and are shaped by those who inhabit them, integrating sensing technologies into urban settings and lifestyles (Kindberg et al., 2007). Paradigms of mobile computing, ubiquitous computing, and pervasive computing have "pushed the notion of anytime, any place connectivity for anyone" (Kortuem and Kawsar, 2010:3). There is increasing recognition of the value of integrating physical infrastructures and digital technologies, creating "smarter" cities which make use of data and analytical techniques to improve efficiency and effectiveness (Gann et al., 2011). "Urban computing" explores how these networked and context-aware technologies can reshape experiences of spatiality, temporality, and embodiment through projected use in everyday places and objects (Galloway, 2004; 2009).

Urban spaces shape the mobility and connectedness of their inhabitants and act as information environments that inhabitants can understand and interpret (Williams and Dourish, 2006). More and more people are engaging with urban computing, yet urban spaces have complex ownership, and have variable densities and usage patterns (Kindberg et al., 2007). Interpretive and reactive urbanized technology—that which can decipher inputs from the surroundings and translate it into outputs and actions1—is becoming inescapable. With it however, a new role emerges for citizen technologists to engage, play with, and shape the urban landscape around them according to their own needs and desires. Information technologies offer citizens new opportunities to participate in urban planning (Hanzi, 2007). Online multiplayer games such as Mudlark's *Chromaroma* allows travelers on the London underground to use their Oystercard RFID data to create a game from their commuting experience (Kiss, 2010). Cities are products of historically and culturally situated practices and flows, where local activities are embedded within processes of cultural production that occur on broader social spaces (Williams and Dourish, 2006), and interventions become shaped by the lived experience of inhabitants within particular environments.

As the name implies, "urban computing" design and technological interventions are framed at the level of the city or district, focusing on sites of clustered activity among citizens as they are brought together to negotiate, engage, interact, and disengage with the city through travel, work, leisure, education, and play. Within cities however, there are homes and these domestic spaces are an overlooked but critical part of the urban landscape. Homes provide the private spaces for people to engage with, hide from, and manage the urban, co-shaping the urban/domestic experience. Inhabitants of cities also inhabit homes and make use of emergent "smart" interconnected technologies such as phones and tablets in both spaces. Technological interventions that allow citizens to negotiate the challenges inherent in public urban environments can, therefore, also be located within private domestic spaces. However, when pervasive computing is applied to the domestic environment, it tends to treat this space as small-scale, isolated, and well-defined (e.g., houses, rooms) (Aldrich, 2003; Kindberg et al., 2007).

Yet domestic behaviors are not isolated, but instead affect urban behaviors and vice versa. Citizens' lived experiences simultaneously encompass both home and city, domestic and urban, yet this concurrence is not recognized in technological interventions. People can gain real-time information about their cities' transport infrastructure while still at home, and information about schools, workplaces, and local environments affect decisions about where to live. Little is known of how ubiquitous technologies might be designed and used within homes by their inhabitants to navigate the intersections of their lives in the city and at home.

In this paper we examine how user innovation and participatory design approaches may be used to develop domestic technological interventions, through the "Homesense" research project. We begin by examining the literatures on users, participatory design, and user innovation, exploring the variable roles for users around innovation and design activities and highlighting how much of the current work in this area focuses on existing communities of practice, despite widespread user innovation in domestic environments. We then draw on these literatures to present the research methodology behind "Homesense," including the use of open-source hardware "toolkits" to facilitate design. We also investigage partnerships that harness "lead user" expertise and use "real" domestic settings as test sites. In the final sections we present the outcomes of the project, and we emphasize that a rich and extensive body of material was gathered from the six research sites over the course of the live phase, the full analysis of which is beyond the scope of this paper. Instead, we focus here on the role of experts and the means in which participants explored the elisions of urban/domestic spaces throughout the project, and we reflect on how successful (or otherwise) this methodology was, discussing the implications for our understanding of user-led innovation

Users, Design, and Innovation

Users of technologies are playing an increasingly important and active role in their design, diffusion, and adoption. Designs fail to gain approval and acceptance when designers have insufficient knowledge about people, their capacities, needs, and desires (Redstrom, 2006), and the most successful innovating firms are those that have close relationships with the users of their products and services (Rothwell et al., 1974). A more active role for the design and development of new technologies has been observed over the past three decades across interdisciplinary research in design studies (Sanders and Stappers, 2008), science and technology studies (Ourdshoorn and Pinch, 2005), and innovation studies (von Hippel, 2005). While increased user involvement has been facilitated by digital and online technologies, there is a longstanding tradition of user engagement in design and innovation activities that should not be considered recent or novel (Voss, 2010).

In design studies, conceptions of collaboration between users and professional designers in "design as an activity" are complex. Different theorists have used different names to describe and classify these activities, including participatory design, co-design, collaborative design, meta design, user-centered, and user-led design. They vary according to the level of user engagement, from user-as-subject to user-as-partner (Sanders and Stappers, 2008). "Participatory design" processes facilitate the active involvement of the people being designed for and other stakeholders in the design process. Here, "users" become active participants in the design process, blurring the boundary between "designer" and "user" (Luck, 2003), and questioning the role of "designer as expert."

Whilst design literatures have focused on design as "purposeful activity" with a goal to make something to be used by someone else (Reich et al., 1996) innovation studies have framed the activities within an economic context, examining the role of firms, the nature of the market, and the necessity of tacit and codified knowledge resources for innovation. The work on user-led innovation describes how individuals, communities, and firms develop products and services for their own use (rather than commercial sale in the first instance) based around knowledge of their own needs and experience, and of the means to provide solutions to those needs (von Hippel, 2005). In contrast to the design literatures the user here is emphatically a partner, collaborator, or even sole inventor/developer of their own innovations. Users are seen to hold "sticky" information about their own needs and preferences which is costly to transfer, making it possible for users to innovate at low costs compared to manufacturers (von Hippel, 1994). The level of user engagement varies according to need, experience, capabilities, and access, with involvement ranging from feedback and support to the full creation of novel products (Flowers et al., 2008). The level of engagement is also shaped by the scale and control of the project. In the large-scale community design of urban spaces, users are expected to take a less active role, participating in the design process through public meetings and workshops (Toker, 2007). Large innovation projects around software are supported through online platforms (that may be provided by firms) and libraries of content, and self-organized communities of individual users (Jeppesen and Fredericksen, 2006).

User-led innovation activities have predominantly been located within communities of practice around professions, extra-curricular activities, and consumer products (e.g., extreme sports [Hiernerth, 2006]; medical practitioners [Lettl et al., 2006]; and open-source software [Lakhani and von Hippel, 2003]). Yet recent research indicates that the most common site of user-led innovation is the home (von Hippel et al., 2010). However, these interventions do not appear to center around the "smart" technologies of pervasive computing (e.g., microcontrollers) but instead around existing artifacts (e.g., cars).

Both urban and domestic settings influence social behaviors (Kindberg et al., 2007) and the user innovation literature highlights how the "sticky information" of lived experience and need can be harnessed into problem solving activities for navigating the urban/domestic interface. Thom-Santinelli (2007) raises concerns that current approaches to urban design and deployment focus on the same privileged groups as designers, potentially leading to digital and material divides between the prosperous and the less prosperous. The user innovation and participatory design approaches offer useful rubrics for examining how technological interventions can be created by the people who will ultimately use them. In the remainder of this paper we draw on these literatures to present the methodology for the "Homesense" research project.

Homesense

The "Homesense" project was developed by Tinker London, with support from EDF R&D, to investigate citizen-led design of reactive and interactive technologies in domestic spaces by bringing open collaboration methods to physical infrastructures in the home. The project was developed in response to perceived failings in the development of "smart" domestic technologies that to date have been seen to adopt top-down approaches, treating the home as a closed social and technological system (Aldrich, 2003). The aim was to explore how better scenarios could develop if users were able to develop products according to their specific needs, social contexts, and lifestyles. To facilitate these user-led innovation practices, the research methodology was developed around three concepts (See Table 1); user-specific needs driving user innovation, the role of "lead user" expertise, and the use of cultural probes in the innovation process. Members of six households across Europe were provided with the tools and resources to build "smart" interactive technologies suited to their own domestic lived experience, through a kit of open-source hardware and a co-located expert. Using these resources, they designed, prototyped, tested, and built their own domestic technological interventions based around their own lived experience over a four to six month "live phase." In the following sections we describe this methodology, and the justification for its development, in greater detail.

User-Specific Needs in the Domestic Space

The location of user-led innovation and design activities is critical. When designing away from the domestic space, designers of consumer technologies bring a

Table 1: Research concepts

Method	Theoretical framing	Timeline
Local expert	"Lead Users" are more innovative than their peers due to possession and integration of valuable types of information (Jeppesen and Laursen, 1999); however, their personal biases might shape the outcomes of design. Non-technical households were, therefore, selected to overcome this bias, and partnered with local "experts" who would provide technical support but not bias the design practice itself.	• Recruitment call, May 2010. • Selection process June–October 2010 • Partnered with suitable household/expert, September–November 2010. • Live phase October 2010–April 2011.
Home as research site	Users design around their own specific need (von Hippel, 2005), but their behaviors and needs are shaped by the specific domestic situation (von Hippel et al., 2010). By siting the design experience within the home over an extended period (4–6 months) users have the potential to develop devices based around the cycle of their daily lives and their unique lived experience.	
ResearchKit	Cultural probes form part of a design-led approach that stresses empathy and engagement (Gaver et al., 1999). A "ResearchKit" of open source hardware electronics enabled users to firstly consider how various aspects of their lived experiences could be made visible and then to develop tangible solutions to domestic needs if so desired.	• Prototype designed, May–June 2010. • User testing, June–July 2010. • Development and manufacture of final ResearchKit, September 2010

reconstructed version of the domestic world into the company, distorting consumer views through frames including gender (Cockburn, 1997). "Smart" interactive technologies are designed outside of homes and are then introduced into homes where residents react to them. This contrasts to an alternative situation where these technologies were designed by occupants themselves (Mayra et al., 2006). To overcome these issues around artificial test environments and separation between the spaces of design, the innovation process was designed to take place by participants *within their own households* over an extended time. This allowed participants to design, test, prototype, and use technologies within the domestic spaces in which they lived (and sometimes worked), which is particularly important in domestic design as users are likely to live in their houses for an extended period and engage with the artifacts within them over a longer time period than in other settings such as hospitals or workplaces.

The "Homesense" project selected six households across four countries—the United Kingdom, Ireland, France, and Switzerland—following an international recruitment campaign, which involved publicizing the project through press releases, online social networks, including Twitter and Facebook, and the real-life social networks of the research team and project partners. Households were selected according to three criteria: household type (comprising housing stock, tenure, location, and composition); prior technological expertise; and proximity

Table 2: Households

Household	Composition	Location	Region	Type
L1	Couple (M, F), one child (M)	London	Owned	Apartment
L2	Couple (M, F)	London	Owned	Apartment
M	Couple (M, F), two children (M, F)	Manchester	Owned	Semi-detached house
K	2 housemates (M, M)	Letterkenny	Rented	Semi-detached house
G	Single occupant (F)	Geneva	Rented	Apartment
P	Single occupant (F)	Paris	Owned	Apartment

to a local "expert." The first two criteria were selected for in the first round of the recruitment process, and "proximity to a local expert" was selected for in the second round.

Domestic behaviors are shaped by household factors including composition (i.e., housemates, partners, children); tenure (i.e., rented, ownership); stock (i.e., old, new-build, apartment, house); and location (i.e., urban, suburban, rural, country) (Druckman and Jackson, 2008). (See Table 2.) Regardless of location of their home, all participants had engagement with urban spaces; members of four of the households both lived and worked in cities, and the participants with homes in suburban and rural locations spent time in local cities for work and leisure.

Lead Users, Expertise, and Proximity

To be able to successfully innovate, users must have solution information and manufacture information. Lead user theory describes how "lead users" are more likely to possess relevant solution information through search and integration of knowledge from different external sources of relevance (Jeppesen and Laursen, 2009). "Lead users" are, therefore, more innovative than other users with regard to new ideas, new applications, and new prototype solutions (Morrison et al., 2000), and also obtain significant benefits from innovating. They are likely to have higher leading-edge status, in-house technical ability, and can be distinguished from non-innovating users (Morrison et al., 2004). However, it is unclear how this technical expertise shapes outcomes of the innovation process itself as technologists have biases in their working strategies (Blackwell et al., 2009). Within the innovation process *who* innovates is critical to kinds of innovations produced (Thom-Santinelli, 2007). Creators of new technologies may imagine themselves as the user—who they are, what they like, what they want.

To limit these biases, households were deliberately selected with limited prior technological experience around electronics. This introduced an interesting set of contradictions to the selection process: suitable households had to be interested and familiar enough with electronics and open source hardware to want to take part in such a project, but not so interested that they already knew how to use them.[2] The households who made the final round of the selection process had all heard of Arduino technologies through friends and colleagues—and in some cases had even bought (or won) some—but hadn't known enough to "get started" with them. This may also reflect the biases of the recruitment process, and in particular the use of personal and technological social networks.

To compensate for this lack of technological experience, the final stage of the selection process involved finding a suitable local "expert" to be partnered with a "household." This provided a means of constructively combining the lived experience of the inhabitants of each specific domestic space, with the technical expertise necessary to develop technological interventions. "Experts" were required to have had prior technological expertise and initiative and were recruited concurrently through similar channels to households, with additional publicity material also sent to several "hackspace" mailing lists and open source hardware online forums. Unexpectedly, four of the six experts recruited also had teaching experience around electronics which proved to be beneficial in the live phase of the project, although it was not something that we had specifically asked for. This final stage of the recruitment process proved to be the most difficult—contrary to our expectations, we received far more "household" applicants than "experts" and had to conduct the final pairing accordingly and many suitable households had to be rejected because we could not find a suitable local "expert."

Design is a social process in which certain factors and activities emerge including: roles and relationships; planning; information gathering; concept generating; and conflict resolution (Cross and Cross, 1995). While it would be both impossible and undesirable to prescribe and control these activities among all participants, roles were clearly defined for both households and experts which were described during the recruitment process, and re-iterated during the training day. While households designed and built (to the best of their abilities) their technology projects, experts used their expertise to provide guidance around the feasibility of the projects and built and coded relevant parts of the projects that were beyond the capabilities of the households. "Experts" were thus deliberately named as such to form their role in terms of the expert technical knowledge that they would bring. Social, familial, and romantic relationships were also present between members of the households (e.g., parents and children; partners) that were also likely to affect the design process.

In participatory design there needs to be a meaningful and productive relationship between "those charged with technology design, and those who must live with its consequences" (Kensing and Blomberg, 1998). Effective communication is a key part of this process (Gallivan and Keil, 2003), not least in facilitating shared understanding of the projects. In the recruitment process, "experts" were deliberately chosen to be physically proximate to their households. This co-location was intended to facilitate the development of a productive and communicative relationship between the household and the experts through the provision of shared experience about the local urban environment, and also to make it easier for both parties to meet during the project.

Probes and Open Source Hardware

To facilitate their activities, each household was provided with a "ResearchKit"—an electronics hardware toolkit consisting of components predominantly composed from the "Arduino" technologies. (See Figure 1.) Like their digital counterparts, the toolkit was intended to make physical interaction and control easily appropriable (Kortuem and Kawsar, 2010). The kit comprised four categories of technologies:

- *Logic and Power*: Arduino board, cables, power supply, sensor shield, keyboard emulator.
- *Digital Inputs*: Push button, touch button, switch, slide switch.

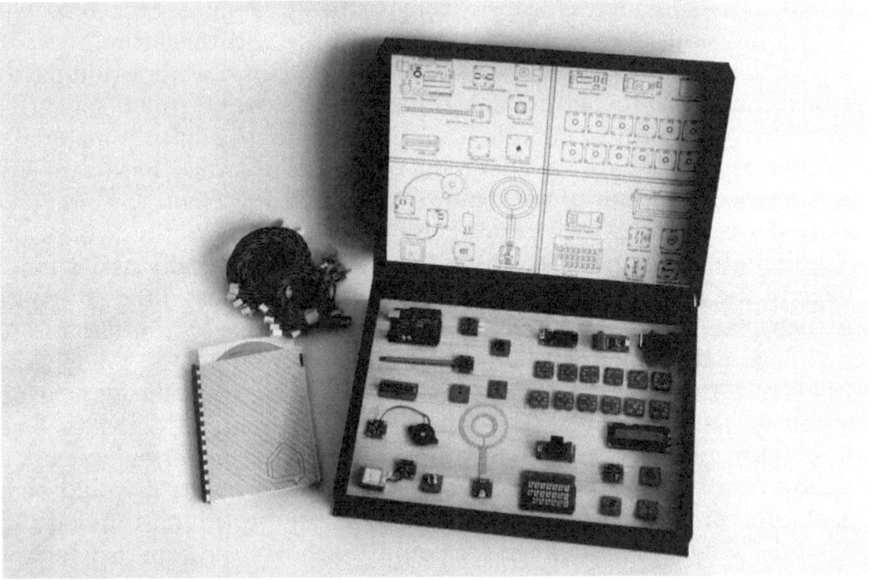

Figure 1: Research Kit

- *Analogue Inputs:* Potentiometer, bend sensor, light sensor, accelerometer, LDR, hall sensor, thermistor, buzzer.
- *Outputs:* LEDs, Servo motor, text LCD.

The ResearchKit was intended to function as a "cultural probe" as part of a design-led approach to understanding the users, stressing empathy and engagement (Gaver et al., 1999). As a probe, the ResearchKit was designed to elicit design inspiration for new domestic technologies (Carolan and Cruickshank, 2011), and, throughout the live phase, make visible the ordinary aspects of their lived domestic lives and engage in conversation with each other, their experts, and the research team to consider how to deal with needs and desires (Graham and Rouncefield, 2008). Despite the technological components of the toolkits, they were not specifically designed as "technology probes" but instead the intent was to make the ordinary details of everyday life visible—for example, visualizing how frequently a participant opened the door of a fridge—and then deciding whether to develop further interventions or not. The "chocolate box" design of the ResearchKit—where the components were arranged by category under a coordinated "lid"—was deliberately chosen to facilitate these considerations by highlighting the potential combinations of inputs and outputs that could be used as starting points for the design process.

"Cultural probes" have been described as a pre-design exercise to elicit ideas (Gaver et al., 1999) to make explicit "sticky information," and to inform further "expert" development and interaction in the design process (Carolan and Cruickshank, 2011). However, the ResearchKit was also designed to enable user-led innovation if participants decided that they would like to take a more active role in further development activities, allowing participants to consider the design of both low- and high-tech interventions. The kit was deliberately constructed around the Arduino microcontroller to facilitate ease of use in non-technical households, a technology which was developed to specifically cater to a non-technical audience by focusing on usability, thereby allowing users to "spend less time figuring out the inner workings and more time experimenting and discovering how it can be used in different environments and scenarios" (Gibb, 2010: 4). Beyond usability, "Arduino" technologies were also deliberately selected due to their open source nature. User involvement in open-source software projects has been well documented (Franke and von Hippel, 2003). By using open-source technologies, it was intended that households and "experts" would not be as constrained in their design activities as they would be if using proprietary hardware, but instead would be able to conduct unrestricted prototyping and experimentation. The Arduino community also provides accessible technology repositories (e.g., code, schematics) and online social forums for support and discussion of projects, providing a further repository of support for households to tap into. Openness—transparency, accessibility, and materiality—matters to members of open-source communities (Balka et al., 2010). Finally, as Thomke and von Hippel (2002: 7) recommend that kits for user-led innovation should "contain libraries of common user modules that can be incorporated into design," a collection of useful code was also developed to allow users to make use of the toolkit without necessarily having to write their own software.

Implementation

Following the selection process, each household engaged in a one-day training exercise in their homes prior to the start of the live phase of the project. This training day had multiple purposes. First, the households were trained by a member of the research team in the use of the Arduino technologies in the ResearchKit. This allowed users to engage more fully in participatory design projects, understanding the issues involved and bridging the gap between their own language and the technical jargon (Reich et al., 1996). The training involved being introduced to each of the Arduino components individually, followed by demonstrations of how each of the categories of technology in the ResearchKit worked together (e.g., input/Arduino board/output). The Processing software and code library were installed onto a computer of the household's choosing, and participants were shown how to install the code onto the Arduino board.

Following the technical training, each household was taken through ideation exercises to help them explore how they inhabited their homes, with questions focusing on what users liked most and least about living in their homes, and how they interacted with the outside world when at home. This led to the development of scenarios about potential projects that households could build. It has been shown that these scenarios can be useful in user-centered design as means of presenting and situating solutions, illustrating alternative solutions, and identifying potential problems (Bodker, 1999). Some of these scenarios were quite specific, while others were more general—the family in one household discussed how a capitalist society and contemporary consumer electronics had already met many of their needs, and what they really wanted was to make the household more "fun."

In the final part of the training, households were introduced to their local "experts." Members of the research team facilitated a discussion about the earlier ideation exercise, and the households and experts co-developed three potential project ideas that they could build during the live phase of the project. The day finished with each household and expert arranging when they would next meet to begin to develop projects. In the case of one household, the training session spilled over into the first development session, and by the time the day ended the team had already built and tested a prototype device that would set a servo-motor to turn off the hallway light after a specific delay, depending on the light intensity.

Data Gathering

As Dourish (2006) notes, ethnographic enquiry allows us to explore the interrelation between the domain of technology and the domain of the everyday, providing insight into the social meanings of technologies. A multi-method ethnographic approach was used in data gathering, and information was collected from each household in an ongoing manner over the course of the live phase through multiple means including interviews, videos, photos, and diaries.

Regular interviews were conducted with both households and experts over the course of the live phase. Face-to-face interviews were conducted with the two households and experts who, like the research team, were London based. Some were conducted at the households' residences which provided an opportunity to directly examine and ask questions about the working projects *in situ*; others took place at other sites including the research team's offices and local coffee shops. To overcome the issues around distance and the potential costs of travel, Skype was used as a means of conducting video interviews and remote online assistance with the far-flung participants in other locations; this was a very effective means of gathering information at distance. The video nature of the technology meant that we were able to gather similar audio and visual information from participants as if we'd interviewed them in person. While phone calls and emails could have been used, Storper and Venables (2004) describe the "buzz" of face-to-face contact as being an important means of information sharing and trust generation; and "face-to-face" contact was particularly important for maintaining good personal relationships with participants who we otherwise would have only seen in person at the beginning and end of the project. When running the program, participants could also use their laptops as live video cameras that they then carried through their households to show off their projects and workspaces.

Cultural probes are also valuable when used with self-reporting behaviors. In addition to interviews, households self-reported their activities through photos, videos and short written reports. Each household was also provided with a small video recorder and encouraged to make short films about their projects. While material from the interviews was kept confidential, self-reported material was used to facilitate the "openness" of the project, and a project website was set up to propagate this information through blog posts. The microblogging site Twitter and the photo sharing platform Flickr were also used by participants and members of the research team to disseminate information and images. Three of the households also used their own personal blogs to present this work. However, this openness led to an unexpected unevenness of reporting. Households who were experiencing difficulties in their projects described how they felt intimidated by the projects that other, more prolific, households were reporting. As a result, they were embarrassed by their own efforts and were hesitant to share information openly about them, although they talked about their own projects freely in interviews. We attempted to counter these feelings with constant encouragement and emphasis that the design process was just as important as the final project outcomes; however, it will be useful for researchers in future "open" projects to be aware of how this type of stage fright might become manifest.

User innovation rarely happens in isolation, but as part of a community effort (Jeppesen and Fredericksen, 2006). While the household-expert relationship had been deliberately set up as part of the research, we also hoped to support the development of relationships *between* the different households and experts, to allow them to support each other and share information about their work. Following discussion about what the best means of contact would be a "Homesense Conversations" Facebook group was set up—however, although all participants could access it, very few made use of it. This may have been because participants were unsure about sharing information with people they hadn't met before—due to the lengthy nature of the recruitment process and the staggering of the start dates for each household, it had not been possible to introduce all 21 participants (13 household members and eight experts) to each other in person before the live phase began. In future work of this nature, it would be useful to get participants to meet as this may encourage and nurture these in-group relationships.

In user-led design projects, effective participation requires continuous commitment and engagement (Reich et al., 1996). In order to facilitate the development of high-salience household technologies, the live phase for each household ran from four to six months. This was to allow sufficient time for users to meet with their experts; plan, design, and develop several projects; and live with the technologies that they had made. Households chose when to end the "live phase" of the study, with every household asking for more time than they had initially planned. A final "exit interview" was conducted with five of the households that documented each project and examined aspects of the overall Homesense project including the use and expansion of the toolkit, the nature of the projects (both successes and failures), learning experiences, and the overall experience of participation and design.

Designing in the Urban/Domestic

"Experts"

At the outset of the project, it had been envisioned that experts would provide a back-up support role, providing both advice about technical aspects of the design process—although not shaping the process itself—and technical support (e.g., writing software if users wanted to extend the ResearchKit; soldering components if necessary). However, the role of the experts varied considerably across each household during the live phase, and experts also took on unforeseen roles. For three of the households, the experts played an active supporting role in the design process. This most commonly involved included writing code for projects once the households had decided what they wanted the devices to do, but only if the household members didn't feel capable of developing this code themselves; and also determining whether the projects that households were proposing were technically feasible or not (where feasibility was defined by their own capabilities).[3] However, experts also assisted in expanding the space—and resources—for development: two of the households were able to make use of the "hackspaces" and personal workshops where their "experts" worked, giving them access to a much wider variety of tools than they otherwise would have had.

These "active" experts emphasized their supporting role in the design and building process—the ideas that were generated came from the needs and experiences of the households themselves, who were encouraged to do as much of the work as possible. These experts also constantly encouraged the households that they were working with to develop technical skills for themselves. For three of the households, the experts took a backseat role. **K** had decided early on in the live phase that he wanted to be as independent as possible and had very little interaction with his expert by choice. Instead he taught himself how to code and successfully developed all of his projects himself. In the remaining two households, the household/expert relationships broke down over the course of the live phase—one expert admitted that he had underestimated the work and time that would be necessary, and did not feel that he had the time or skills. For both of these households, the research team attempted to provide adequate support to compensate for this loss but also encouraged the household to see how far they could progress on their own. While both households persisted in their efforts, they described how they felt somewhat lost and unprepared without having a reliable expert to turn to, which in turn undermined their confidence in their abilities to design and develop devices. As the role of the experts and the degree of the support that they provided varied by household, so too did the activities of the households. In some instances, households built original devices with little outsider help; in others, households and experts collaborated together to develop working prototypes.

The interactions between all experts and households were also limited by the time that they were able to spend together and, with the exception of the Geneva-based participants (where the household members and experts lived comparably near to each other), all participants described their difficulties in being able to coordinate a time when they could spend a couple of hours together to work. This raises questions about whether "physically proximate" also constitutes "co-location" when considering design in domestic spaces. For some of the activities in the design process, such as coding, participants felt that there was no need to be near each other (and indeed talked of "emailing the code over"). However, when discussing the design interventions that were being planned within their home, many participants felt that it was important for their expert to be in the same space so they could see and understand how the intervention was going to work; and in some instances, be involved in practical aspects such as taking measurements, determining where the fuse box was, etc. In other instances, both experts and household members also wanted to meet in the same hackspace or workshop so that they could work on building the devices together; again, with the expectation that the households would ultimately be able to learn how to work with electronic artifacts in the future.

Devices in the Urban/Domestic

The devices which households imagined, and sometimes built, explored what was meant by domestic space. Some projects focused exclusively on behavior of participants within the "inside" environment of their homes. These included the

"Kettle Switch" developed by **L2** which was intended to save time in the mornings—the device incorporated a light sensor, a servo motor and rudimentary cardboard casing and switch which turned the kettle in the kitchen on when the light was switched on. Other projects were conceived around the elisions between behavior in the domestic and behavior in the wider urban environment, four of which are documented below.

Project 1: "Milk Monitor." This device was conceived in the early part of **L2**'s live phase, with both members of the household describing how they would frequently run out of milk, and how annoying it was to have to leave their apartment and go out into Central London at night to buy more. The original plan had been to build a device that would use a light detector to measure how much milk was left in the container in the fridge; once the level fell below a certain amount, the device would then send a message to **L2**s' phones reminding them to buy more. This would send data between the domestic and the urban, encouraging behavior in the urban (buying milk) that would benefit behavior in the domestic (drinking tea). However, the practicalities of actually building the device proved too difficult—in particular, it was unlikely to fit in the slim shelf inside the fridge where the milk container was placed—and the idea was abandoned.

Project 2: "Rest In Peace." **G** designed a device that was intended to "make the lives of my neighbors a little easier" as she lived in an old apartment complex with thin walls, and was concerned about disturbing her elderly neighbor when she had friends over or played her music. She and her two experts discussed the possibility of developing a device that would let her know when the noise levels in her apartment rose above a certain point, and based on this information, her experts wrote software that linked different levels of noise to certain colors of LEDs (i.e., green = quiet; yellow = medium; red = loud). They also built a "little circuit with an electric microphone and a simple operational amplifier" and the three of them tested it together at **G**'s apartment. When they had all determined that these components were functional, **G** built a casing for the device using brightly colored Lego bricks that fitted the aesthetic of the blinking LEDs. While the device was designed to shape **G**'s behavior *within* her apartment, it recognized that this was in turn driven by concerns of how this was affected by outside factors (i.e., her concern about the well-being of her neighbors, the structural composition of her apartment block).

Project 3: "Bike Map." The "Bike Map" was developed by **L1** over the course of the live phase. **L1**'s apartment in Central London was near three "bike stations" for the "Barclays' Cycle Hire" scheme. Although the members of **L1** wanted to make more use of this cycle scheme, it was frustrating not to know exactly which of the stations had the most bikes and described how they had made several wasted journeys out of their apartment and around several of the stations until they found a bike to use. The device consisted of an Arduino board, a WiFi Shield, green LEDs, and a map of the area around **L1**'s apartment presented in a simple frame from Muji. (See Figure 2.) It analyzed data available from the Cycle Hire scheme to determine how many bikes were at each station—when more than five bikes were available, the LED at the appropriate station lit up. **L1** described it as a "glanceable guide" that could be placed by the door in the apartment and was simpler than having to find and load the

Figure 2: Bike Map

relevant app on their smart devices. The idea was developed by **L1**, who assisted their experts in the development of the code. The aesthetic appearance of the device was also deliberately designed by **L1** to appear simple and low-tech, fitting in with the existing décor of their home.

Project 4: "The Angry Bin." This gadget was developed by **K** as a means of reminding him and his housemate to put more of their waste material in the recycling containers and less in the "main" bin. The device consists of a white resin "case" with a face on it, and was fixed to the top of the main bin. As the lid of the bin was lifted, the device rotated from a "happy" face to a progressively more "angry" face every time the lid was lifted. All parts of Angry Bin—hardware and software—were developed by **K** alone. He designed the shape of the casing, printed it out on a 3D-printer at his workplace (although he admitted later than he wasn't happy about the face); and also wrote the software which linked the rotation of the "face" to the lifting motion, before assembling all of the components to create the final device. Like "Rest in Peace", Angry Bin was designed to shift **K's** (and his housemate's) behavior *within* his home—separating out the recycling—as a response to factors *outside* his home (i.e., protecting the environment).

The domestic/urban divide also shaped the ways in which some projects were brought to fruition, or not. **G** had originally conceived of a device notionally called *"IN-> OUT communication (broadcast my life),"* which would use LED panels placed in her apartment's windows to broadcast to the outside based on events inside her home such as "my fridge is empty." However, this was abandoned after **G** realized that this device could also potentially advertise her presence and absence to burglars.

Conclusion

Pervasive technologies highlight the artificial construction of boundaries between urban and domestic spaces. In this paper we have highlighted the importance of considering domestic spaces as part of the wider urban environment. We have presented a method to facilitate participatory and user-led innovation in domestic spaces, in a way that also takes the greater urban environment in which these homes are situated into account. As individuals inhabit both complex worlds they have unique sets of needs that we believe can be effectively harnessed and met though participatory user-led interventions. By involving domestic users in this design process, we also hope to stop the biases of designers and their demographics inherent in urban design (Thom-Santinelli, 2007).

By enabling in-home development, the methodology allowed participants to design and build in the space that the interventions were designed for—both the domestic space and the urban environment around it—rather than in an artificial test environment that did not embody either of the above locations. The devices and solutions developed by participants demonstrated the porous nature of their homes, highlighting how domestic solutions are not constrained to "domestic" problems but instead shape and are shaped by the wider environment. Interventions intended to alter behaviors in urban spaces can draw on data from the home (e.g., "Milk Monitor"), and vice versa (e.g., "Bike Map"). The interventions also raise questions about where the boundaries of the home and the cityscape lie—in nearby homes ("Rest in Peace"), local areas ("Milk Monitor," "Bike Map"), or the wider environment ("Angry Bin"). The "Bike Map" also demonstrates the potential power of open data provision, such as that provided by the Barclays Cycle Hire scheme, in providing means to develop connectivity between information environments (Williams and Dourish, 2006). Yet the project also demonstrates how the urban can curtail the domestic—the potential risks behind the "broadcast my life" project has interesting parallels with the ways in which other digital location-based technologies have also been linked to criminal opportunism (Bloxham, 2011).

The research method also recognized that homes themselves are not isolated physical sites that expertise can be parachuted into—instead, the co-location of "experts" provided a way of facilitating the design process between households and experts, and also a shared understanding of the wider urban environment. However, the physical space of the city also shaped these relationships, influencing how long it took for participants to cross the city to see each other and even the physical difficulties in transporting delicate electronics equipment via public transport from one site to another. In developing this type of research methodology further, it would be useful to consider how such elements of design activities are enabled, or constrained, by the urban space in which they take place.

Access to resources is critical to innovation activities, and the "Homesense" methodology provided both tangible and tacit knowledge-based resources to participants via the ResearchKit and local experts. This combination allowed participants to explore a spectrum of user-led innovation and participatory design activities, based around their own experiences, capabilities, and needs. Dourish (2006) criticizes probes for being a form of "discount ethnography" when used alone, because they fail to capture the coupling of analytic and methodological concerns. However, this work shows that when used in parallel with other concepts that specifically work with theoretical frameworks such as lead users and "sticky knowledge," "probes" have the potential to explore both theoretical and empirical avenues of interest. It would be useful for future work to explore the ResearchKit's elision between the "probe" approach and the "toolkits" that are described in the user innovation literature (e.g., Thomke and von Hippel, 2002).

In addition to the provision of distinct resources, the pairing of multiple methods of data collection and visual communication technologies such as Skype was also successful. These technologies allowed the research team to maintain relationships with participants and gather complex data from several dispersed research sites at great geographical distance. Social networking technologies also enabled information to be shared about the project as it progressed through the voices of the participants themselves. However, we also caution about how "open" such research can ever be. As Dourish (2006) notes, ethnography is not a passive agent and ethnographic data is not unproblematically extracted from a setting but through an encounter between that setting and the ethnographer. In "Homesense" the research team took care to differentiate between information about the technologies that participants developed, and information about the participants themselves. Yet the social nature of the project—where relationships were set up between experts and participants, between the different research sites, and between the research sites and the research team—combined with the openness of reporting led to participants comparing themselves with each other and being selective about which data they revealed in a public forum. We, therefore, caution future researchers to recognize the biases that may emerge around data reporting in open research projects, particularly those with a social element—and advise that private data also be collected to complement that which is available in the public domain.

Away from the controlled environment of a test lab, user-led innovation and participatory design in the urban/domestic realm is a complex and multifaceted process encompassing variant factors around lived experience, technical experience, and confidence; where design activities and capabilities, whether collaborative or user-led, are not fixed but instead evolve over time and through space. The "Homesense" project has shown that "home" does not stop inside the front door, nor does the "city" halt outside it. Technological interventions around them must bridge and inhabit both spaces such that "street computing" does not simply embody a pavement alongside a main road, but a pathway that runs from the heart of the city to the heart of the home.

Notes

1. An example of a reactive interpretive technology is the "Nazbagtag", a wifi-enabled wireless device in the shape of a rabbit which is manufactured by Violet. Nazbagtags can connect to the internet to receive and transmit data and can also react to the information in several ways (e.g., lighting up, moving its ears, "speaking").
2. Despite explicitly stating the selection criteria in the publicity for the project, we also received several applications from individuals with extensive professional experience as engineers; however, we also invited several of them to reapply as "experts" instead.
3. For example, G's experts spent some time developing code for one of the proposed projects before deciding that it was beyond the scope of their capabilities.

Note on Contributors

Georgina Voss is a research fellow at the Faculty of Arts, Brighton University, and an honorary research associate at the Science and Technology Studies Department, University College London.

Natasha Carolan is a doctoral candidate at the HighWire Centre, Lancaster University, and "Chief Elf" at Makielab, London.

Bibliography

F. Aldrich, "Smart Homes: Past, Present, Future," in R. Harper, ed., *Inside the Smart Home* (London: Springer-Verlag, 2003).

K. Balka, C. Raasch, and H. Herstatt, "Open Source Innovation: A Study of Openness and Community Expectations," paper presented at the DIME Conference, (Milano, April, 14—16, 2010).

A. Blackwell, J. Rode, and E. Toye, "How Do We Program the Home? Gender, Attention Investment and the Psychology of Programming at Home," *International Journal of Human Computer Studies* 67:4 (2009) 324–341.

A. Bloxham, "Most Burglars using Facebook and Twitter to Target Victims, Survey Suggests," *The Telegraph* (26 September 2011) 21.

S. Bodker, "Scenarios in User-Center Design—Setting the Stage for Reflection and Action," *Proceedings of the 32nd Hawaii International Conference on System Sciences* (1999).

N. Carolan and L. Cruickshank, "Understanding Design Interventions in Democratic Innovation: A Toolkit Approach," *Design Research Journal* 2:10 (2011) 33–38.

C. Cockburn, "Domestic Technologies: Cinderella and the Engineers," *Women's Studies International Forum* 20 (1997) 361–371.

N. Cross and A. Cross, "Observations of Teamwork and Social Processes in Design," *Design Studies* 16 (1995) 143–170.

P. Dourish, "Implications for Design," *CHI2006 Proceedings: Design: Creative and Historical Perspectives* (2006).

A. Druckman and T. Jackson, "Household Energy Consumption in the UK: A Highly Geographically And Socio-Economically Disaggregated Model," *Energy Policy* 36 (2008) 3177–3192.

S. Flowers, J. Mateos-Garcia, J. Sapsed, P. Nightingale, A. Grantham, and G. Voss, *The New Inventors: How Users are Changing the Rules of Innovation* (London: NESTA, 2008).

N. Franke and E. von Hippel, "Satisfying Heterogeneous User Needs via Innovation Toolkits: The Case of Apache Security Software," *Research Policy* 32 (2003) 1199–1215.

M. Gallivan and M. Keil, "The User-Development Communication Process: A Critical Case Study," *Information Systems Journal* 13 (2003) 37–68.

A. Galloway, "Intimations of Everyday Life: Ubiquitous Computing and the City," *Cultural Studies* 18 (2004) 384–408.

A. Galloway, "A Brief History of the Future of Urban Computing and Locative Media" (PhD thesis, Carleton University, 2009).

D. Gann, M. Dodgson, and D. Bhardwaj, "Physical-Digital Interaction in City Infrastructure," *IBM Journal of Research and Development* 55:8 (2011) 1–10.

B. Gaver, T. Dunne, and E. Pacenti, "Design: Cultural Probes," *Interactions* 6 (1999) 21–29.

A. Gibb, "New Media, Art, Design, and the Arduino Microcontroller: A Malleable Tool," unpublished Master's thesis, Pratt Institute (2010).

C. Graham and M. Rouncefield, "Probes and Participation," paper presented at Participatory Design Conference, (Bloomington, IN, 30 September–4 October, 2008).

M. Hanzi, "Information Technology as a Tool for Public Participation in Urban Planning: A Review of Experiments and Potential," *Design Studies* 28 (2007) 289–307.

C. Hienerth, "The Commercialization of User Innovations: The Development of the Rodeo Kayak Industry," *R&D Management* 36 (2006) 273–294.

L. Jeppesen and L. Frederiksen, "Why Do Users Contribute to Firm-Hosted User Communities? The Case of Computer-Controlled Music Instruments," *Organization Science* 17 (2006) 45–64.

L. Jeppesen and K. Laursen, "The Role of Lead Users in Knowledge Sharing," *Research Policy* 38 (2009) 1582–1589.

F. Kensing and J. Blomberg, "Participatory Design: Issues and Concerns," *Computer Supported Co-operative Work* 7 (1998) 167–185.

T. Kindberg, A. Chalmers, and E. Paulos, "Urban Computing," *IEEE Pervasive Computing* 40 (2007) 18–20.

J. Kiss, "Chromaroma: The Makeover London Commuting Has Been Waiting For," *Guardian Digital Content Blog* (30 November 2010), <http://www.guardian.co.uk/media/pda/2010/nov/30/chromaroma-oyster-transport-gaming> Accessed August 12, 2012.

G. Kortuem and F. Kawsar, "Market-Based User Innovations in the Internet of Things," *IEEE* (2010) 1–8.

K. Lakhani and E. von Hippel, "How Open Source Software Works: 'Free' User-To-User Assistance," *Research Policy* 32 (2003) 923–943.

C. Lettl, C. Herstatt, and H. Gemuenden, "Users' Contributions to Radical Innovation: Evidence from Four Cases in the Field of Medical Equipment Technology," *R&D Management* 36 (2006) 251–272.

R. Luck, "Dialogue in Participatory Design," *Design Studies* 24 (2003) 523–535.

F. Mayra, A. Soronen, I. Koskinen, K. Kuusela, J. Mikkonen, J. Vanhala, and M. Zakrzewski, "Probing a Proactive Home: Challenges in Researching and Designing Everyday Smart Environments," *Human Technology* 2 (2006) 158–186.

P. Morrison, J. Roberts, and D. Midgely, "The Nature of Lead Users and Measurement of Leading-edge Status," *Research Policy* 33 (2004) 351–362.

P. Morrison, J. Roberts, and E. von Hippel, "Determinants of User Innovation and Innovation Sharing in a Local Market," *Management Science* 46 (2000) 1513–1527.

N. Oudshoorn and T. Pinch, *How Users Matter: The Co-Construction of Users and Technology* (Cambridge, MA: MIT Press, 2005).

J. Redstrom, "Towards User Design? On the Shift from Object to User as the Subject of Design," *Design Studies* 27 (2006) 123–139.

Y. Reich, S. Konda, I. Monarch, S. Levy, and E. Subrahmanian, "Varieties and Issues of Participation and Design," *Design Studies* 17 (2006) 165–180.

R. Rothwell, C. Freeman, A. Horlsey, V. Jervis, A. Robertson, and J. Townsend, "SAPPHO Updated – Project SAPPHO Phase II," *Research Policy* 3 (1974) 258–291.

E. Sanders and P. Stappers, "Co-Creation and the New Landscapes of Design," *CoDesign* 4 (2008) 5–18.

M. Storper and A. Venables, "Buzz: Face-To-Face Contact and the Urban Economy," *Journal of Economic Geography* 4:4 (2004) 351–370.

S. Thomke and E. von Hippel, "Customers as Innovators: A New Way to Create Value," *Harvard Business Review* 80:4 (2002) 74–81.

J. Thom-Santelli, "Mobile-Social Software: Facilitating Serendipity or Encouraging Homogeneity?" *IEEE Pervasive Computing* 6:3 (2007) 46–51.

Z. Toker, "Recent Trends in Community Design: The Eminence of Participation," *Design Studies* 28 (2007) 309–323.

E. von Hippel, "'Sticky Information' and the Locus of Problem Solving: Implications for Innovation," *Management Science* 40 (1994) 429–439.

E. von Hippel, *Democratizing Innovation* (Cambridge MA: MIT Press, 2005).

E. von Hippel, J. de Jong, and S. Flowers, "Comparing Business and Household Sector Innovation in Consumer Products: Findings from a Representative Study in the UK," Working Paper (2010) <http://papers.ssrn.com> Accessed August 12, 2012.

G. Voss, "The Historical Construction of User Innovation," in S. Flowers and F. Henwood, eds., *Perspectives on User Innovation* (London: Imperial College Press, 2010).

A. Williams and P. Dourish, "Imagining the City: The Cultural Dimensions of Urban Computing," *IEEE Pervasive Computing* 39 (2006) 38–43.

Enabling the Real-Time City: LIVE Singapore!

Kristian Kloeckl, Oliver Senn and Carlo Ratti

ABSTRACT *The increasing pervasiveness of urban systems and networks utilizing digital technologies for their operation generates enormous amounts of digital traces capable of reflecting in real-time how people make use of space and infrastructures in the city. This is not only transforming how we study, design, and manage cities but opens up new possibilities for tools that give people access to up-to-date information about urban dynamics, allowing them to take decisions that are more in sync with their environment. This paper documents the ongoing LIVE Singapore! project which explores the development of an open platform for the collection, elaboration and distribution of a large and growing number of different kinds of real-time data that originate in a city. Inspired by recent data.gov initiatives, the platform is structured to become itself a tool for developer communities, allowing them to analyze data and write applications that create links between a city's different real-time data streams, offering new insights and services to citizens. Being a compact island based city-state metropolis, Singapore offers a unique context for this study. This paper addresses the value of stream data for city planning and management as well as modalities to give citizens meaningful access to large amounts of data capable of informing their decisions. We describe the technology context within which this project is framed, illustrate the requirements and the architecture of the open real-time data platform to serve as a base for programming the city, and finally we present and discuss the first platform prototype (using real-world data from operators of cellphone networks, taxi fleet, public transport, sea port, airport, and others). Based on this prototype a public showcasing of the project was staged in April 2011 at the Singapore Art Museum and the visual data analytics generated are illustrated in the paper. Finally, we draw some conclusions of technical as well as organizational nature regarding the challenges we faced when working in new ways with real-world, real-time data streams in an urban context that will help inform further development of our as well as of related projects in progressing in disclosing the potential of the wealth of digital data generated by urban systems, networks, and infrastructures.*

Introduction

Think of an encounter with a friend you ran into on the street. You both stop and exchange information—greetings, personal anecdotes, the weather, etc. In telling this story you formulate the phrases on the basis of your knowledge of the subject, as well as your knowledge of your friend's background. When he frowns his eyebrows, you understand that he disagrees; his gesture informed you he wanted to intervene and respond. You respond with a pause to give him an opportunity to contribute to the discussion. You note that your friend is getting impatient to finish the discussion when he looks at his watch. He, in turn, sees that you have noticed his impatience and explains he has an appointment to go to. All this interaction happens—in real-time. Your senses are capable of understanding this dynamic of interaction in a very effective way when the signals necessary for such an interaction can be perceived and when the signals are strong enough to be picked up.

Real-time interaction between people and these dynamics, instead, become difficult when distances between the person and the relevant phenomena grow (think of the size of a city) or when signals are of a kind that human senses have difficulty picking up or interpreting (think of pollutants contained in the air you breath). Now, consider the potential of allowing people's decisions to be informed by those phenomena, rendering dynamics on an urban scale as efficient and effective as that discussion between you and your friend.

Over the past years, urban space has been pervaded by networks and systems that generate digital bits. These bits are closely related to human activity, both informing human actions as well as reflecting their effects. Accessing the Internet on a laptop from a café locates the user through the WiFi antenna, using a cell phone registers at the nearest antenna tower, an online search or order of a product online establishes countless histories describing your preferences and interests, using a public transport smart card generates records on the origin and destination patterns of your trip, these, to name but a few examples, create a digital trace of your activity. This generation of bits happens incidentally, being generated and memorized during the daily acts of a city's life, and as such has the potential to reveal the complex facets of the city and its inhabitants in detail and in real-time (Rojas, Kloeckl, and Ratti, 2008). The increasing pervasiveness of urban systems and networks using digital technologies generates enormous numbers of digital traces capable of reflecting, in real-time, how people make use of space and infrastructures in the city. This is not only transforming how we study, design, and manage cities but opens up new possibilities for tools that give people access to up-to-date information about urban dynamics, allowing individuals to make decisions that are more in sync with their environment.

However, most digitally managed urban systems generate data for the purpose of their own operations and do not make those data directly accessible to other urban systems or the public. As a result, digital bits describing human activity in urban space related to these systems are accurately described by the generated data but locked within each of these specific domains. In the LIVE Singapore! Project, we are now exploring the development of an open platform for the collection, combination, and distribution of large numbers of a city's real-time data, allowing developer communities to join in creating applications that turn these data streams into meaningful and beneficial tools for people to make use of in their cities.

We have articulated this article in the following structure:

- LIVE Singapore!—The Project
  - Singapore: an ideal real-time city?
  - open data initiatives and platforms

  - mash-ups and combining data
  - an open platform project
  - users creating connections among data
  - feedback loops
  - system pictures
- Architecture for an Urban Real-Time Data Platform
  - data transport requirements
  - platform architecture
  - aspects of scalability and flexibility
  - data processing functionality
  - a first implementation and evaluation of a platform prototype
  - aspects of data format and semantics
  - LIVE Singapore! Exhibiting An Urban Demo
  - Critical Issues
  - Where Are We and What Is Next?

LIVE Singapore!—The Project

The SENSEable City Lab, housed at the Massachusetts Institute of Technology, has over the past years created partnerships with entities that manage large urban systems whose normal operation generates large data streams, and we have developed innovative ways of interpreting these and inferring urban activity as it happens in real-time. The Real-Time Rome project (Calabrese et al., 2007) analyzed data streams originating from Italy's largest cellphone network and from GPS locations of Rome's public transport bus fleet and its taxi fleet. The project's objective was to explore how using real-time data could allow for the better planning and managing of cities, with the main audience being planners and architects. A year later, Real-time Rome was succeeded by the WikiCity project (Calabrese et al., 2007) in which our work with real-time data was taken further, exploring a way in which combinations of data streams could be turned into effective tools for citizens to support the decision making process when following their goals and activities in the city.

The LIVE Singapore! project builds on these initiatives and takes them a step further. The project is not geared to any limited number of applications of real-time data in the city nor does it single out a few data streams; rather it develops a platform that is made accessible to developers in the city and beyond to share in making novel combinations and uses of a growing number of available urban data streams.

Over the past years significant work has been carried out in the domain of urban sensing such as that described in the CitySense initiative (Murty et al., 2008; Paulsen and Riegger, 2006). In these cases, sensor networks are deployed ad hoc, allowing for a high level of control of the forms of data generated by the system. Other projects, predominantly in the transportation domain (such as Massachusetts Bay Transportation Authority (MBTA) open data on real time bus locations), focus on making available existing data streams while remaining predominantly within one single type of data generated by one network.

In the LIVE Singapore! Project, we acknowledge that vast amounts of data are being generated in growing numbers of diverse urban systems as a kind of by-product of the specific system's operations. These data have the potential to reveal urban dynamics that go beyond the sole system of origin. Furthermore, such data often represent large parts of a city's population (consider the 143.6 percent cellphone penetration rate in Singapore as an example [IDA Singapore, 2012]), and in this way refers to a new urban context in which the daily reality of the city's inhabitants becomes the center of interest, as described by Zardini (2006). In this sense, LIVE Singapore! does not set out to solve any one specific urban issue as such but rather explores the development of new digital tools that enable radically new approaches to how urban issues can be addressed.

Singapore: An Ideal Real-Time City?

Singapore is in many ways an ideal setting for the exploration and experimentation of an open real-time data platform. Singapore is a city state and as such all territory is one city, both in terms of its dynamics as well as in terms of political administration—this is of great help in identifying and engaging with relevant partners for collaborations. Singapore's 5,076,700 inhabitants (2010 Census) live in an area covering only 710.2 km^2 of surface area. It is an island connected with the Malaysian mainland via only two bridges for motorized traffic; all other passenger and freight transportation is managed either via sea or via air traffic, with Changi Airport being a significant hub in the southeast Asian region and Singapore's container port being the world's second largest container port as well as the largest transshipment container port in the world. In this context, Singapore is a highly developed city, with advanced infrastructures and networks and in a tech savvy population familiar with recent developments in electronic mobile devices. Additionally, Singaporeans are familiar with rapid radical change in their city structure considering the country's rapid development since its independence in 1965 both in economic as well as in infrastructural terms: Singapore's annual GDP at current market prices has increased from US$ 1,919 million in 1970 to US$ 259,823 million in 2010 (Singapore Department of Statistics, 2012), while the city's subway system, opened only in 1987, has now expanded to four lines, 84 stations and 130km (Singapore Land Transport, 2012).

For all the above Singapore provides an ideal context for exploring research and development aspects connected to an urban, real-time data platform. It being so ideally suited, the risk is rather that not all discoveries and developments will likely be directly replicable in other urban contexts.

Open Data Initiatives and Platforms

LIVE Singapore! is inspired by the recent developments in the field of open data initiatives. In May 2009 the U.S. government launched the first of what has since been referred to as data.gov (data.gov, 2011) initiatives in which it made non-sensitive historic data sets publicly available in order to increase the "ability of the public to easily find, download, and use datasets that are generated and held by the Federal Government" (data gov, 2011). In this dynamic of giving data collected from the people back to the people, some of the goals are to spur economic, scientific, and educational innovation, and to promote citizen participation, as well as to drive down government costs by inviting a larger public community to actively participate in exploring how new value can be created from existing sets of data and their novel combinations. Since its start, the initiative has been replicated in various other countries (the United Kingdom) and cities (London and San Francisco) and multiple applications have been created based upon the data sets made available through these platforms.

Not limited to public data sources, platform projects such as Pachube (Pachube, 2011) have tackled the challenge of sharing sensor data over the web ("data brokerage"). The project was developed as an infrastructure for the Internet of Things that allows individuals and organizations/companies to make their sensor data available online. The platform uses a RESTful, HTTP-based API for the interaction among the sensors, the platform, and the clients which makes it easy to publish and consume sensor data.

Two different ways are supported for uploading data. The sensor can directly "push" data by issuing a HTTP PUT request along with the data. Alternatively, Pachube can also poll data from the sensor in 15-minute intervals or when a user is requesting data (if the sensor is supporting this mode). Pachube primarily focuses on supporting sensors with low sampling rates, since both mechanisms to upload data are based on HTTP requests and, therefore, are not suited for high-rate data streams.

Apart from acting as a data exchange platform between sensors and clients, Pachube does not provide any data processing functionality such as aggregation, advanced filtering, or combination of data streams.

Mashups and Combining Data

In a Web context, Mashup applications combine two or more sources of data to create a certain functionality or to simply derive new data sets. Mashup tools help in acquiring, combining, filtering, and aggregating the data. Furthermore, often these tools allow users to easily build (i.e., without programming skills) mashups and visualize or share the outcome of the mashup process.

One example of an online mashup tool is Yahoo Pipes (Yahoo Pipes, 2011). In analogy to Unix pipes, the idea is to apply several simple operators after each other to one or more data sources in order to extract the data that is needed. The tool supports several mechanisms to fetch data such as reading from CSV files, accessing RSS and Atom feeds or getting images from Flickr (an image hosting website). Yahoo Pipes does, however, not offer mechanisms to fetch data from data streams; it only polls the data sources in certain time intervals.

Once the data is loaded, different operators can be used to modify and combine data from different sources. There are separate operators that filter, sort, and aggregate data. To build the mashups, users employ a visual editor rather than a query or scripting language. After the mashup is finished, it can be viewed and reused by other users.

The functionality of Yahoo Pipes allows users to quickly combine various static data sets. The goal in LIVE Singapore is to have similar functionality but for real-time data streams. This increases the complexity of the operators significantly since data streams are infinite streams of messages but most operators (say the sort operator) rely on a limited set of messages with which to work.

An Open Platform Project

The LIVE Singapore! project leverages all of the above described dynamics. It is a flexible and scalable open platform structure enabling the collection, combination, as well as the distribution of large and growing numbers of real-time data streams originating from a city. Inspired by the data.gov initiatives, LIVE Singapore! is not a limited set of specific applications as such but an enabling platform on top of which developer communities, internal as well as external to the project group, can subsequently build applications that employ combinations of the data feeds available through the platform. In this way, instead of limiting the application development to a restrained group, we trigger a dynamic of crowd sourcing of the actual ideas created and the development of applications that become possible for the city, firmly believing in the creative potential of cities and their inhabitants. As in the case of the data.gov initiatives and their historic datasets, also in this project's context, letting citizens, city planners, companies, authorities actively work with live data streams has the objective of: fostering crowd sourcing, multiplying the creative potential, and ultimately setting the base for an emerging economy based on new ways to extract value from data. For this reason, the LIVE Singapore! platform aims at becoming somewhat an ecosystem with toolboxes that enable developers to write applications that turn urban real-time data into useful information for citizens.

While working with real-time data from any one single technology network has shown interesting results in recent years, it is becoming increasingly clear how the combination of very different types of data can bring about even richer insights into how cities work and how people make use of space. The data that we are considering for this project can be divided into three groups: data as a "by-product" from existing networks, data collected with tags or sensors, and data actively shared by people.

Dealing actively with a multitude of data that originate from very differently structured networks brings one main attention to the conception of connector elements as outlined in the next section. While we are actively developing code to include data streams in this first prototype phase, we will be moving towards providing indications as to how external data providers can provide data to the platform in a more standardized way. It is clear that a platform such as LIVE Singapore! needs to tackle and resolve the seemingly conflicting requirements of providing connectors that require as little data processing and conversion on the provider side as possible (in order not to discourage participation), yet receives data streams that are as coherently structured and described as possible for a maximum of interoperability and the possibility of combining different data streams. Striking a balance is a challenge well known in the study of system change:

> If connections are too few, networks are frozen and no change occurs, and if connections are too many, there is no stability and networks remain chaotic. Along the margin between too little and too much connection, 'the spontaneous emergence of self-sustaining webs' occurs,

says Mark Taylor (Taylor, 2001: 148), quoting biologist Stuart Kauffman.

By creating a platform that enables previously impossible or hard-to-achieve links among diverse data streams, LIVE Singapore increases the complexity of the urban system, since "complexity is directly related to connectivity. As connections or interconnections proliferate, complexity expands and, correlatively, information increases" (Taylor, 2001:139). And this increase of complexity, of connections among elements which in this case are data streams originating from very diverse sources in the city, is what the project ultimately aims at: creating a platform for developers to connect multiple and diverse data streams, generating in this way unprecedented insights into a city's dynamics as well as developing tools and applications for citizens to navigate through them and act upon them in a way that is constructive for both their individual as well as collective goals.

For this reason, another of the platform's declared requirements that orients development is to provide easy access and easy programmability in order to capture as large as possible an active developer audience, interested and able to program applications that valorize the available data streams.

Users Creating Connections among Data

Currently, much of the value that is being attributed to many online platform projects is the data that these platforms accumulate and which give them deep insights into their user's activities and preferences. The situation for LIVE Singapore! is of a fundamentally different nature: This project deals with stream data and as such does not store any data within the platform—it is always the data provider that has control over what data is made available. We believe it would be difficult for any one operator to propose itself today to centrally host a wide variety of a city's data streams for difficulties related to data management performance but even more so for questions of data ownership, privacy, and security. The platform is, therefore, structured to make data streams available in a coherent form but not to store these data. Historic data can be made available in much the same way as the live streams, being hosted on the providers' site and made available through connectors via the platform.

LIVE Singapore! in this way sees the value of data not in it's centralized accumulation but focuses on keeping track of the connections made between real-time data streams by developers and users creating applications. While the semantics of data streams is a challenge, even more so is the semantics of data connections: what is the value and meaning of the combination of any group of data streams? Our approach lets the users make and describe these connections while saving this information within the platform in order to gradually grow an internal knowledge about the semantics of stream connections to inform the platform's growth.

Feedback Loops

We have indicated above how people's actions in cities translate into data in multiple technology systems. Providing information on urban dynamics (gained through the collection and analysis of those data) to people when they are in the process of making decisions, creates new and effective feedback loops to the city system:

> In an information-feedback system, conditions are converted to information that is a basis for decisions that control action to alter the surrounding conditions. The cycle is continuous. We cannot properly speak of any beginning or end of the chain. It is a closed loop. (Forrester, 1961: 61)

While it is certainly still the case that in such a system "it is always the presently available information about the past which is being used as a basis for deciding future action" (Forrester, 1961: 15), working with real-time data today as described does move that past significantly closer to the present and can reduce delay, allowing for more timely and potentially effective decisions and actions. While Forrester points out that delays in systems do not necessarily have a negative role but can also have a stabilizing one, the feasibility of shorter delays does open up new possibilities and increases the flexibility with which delay time in feedback loops in urban dynamics can be put to use for more effective employment of resources and energy in the city.

Important questions emerge regarding the impact that such new real-time feedback loops will have on a city and on its dynamics—will they break the stability of the system? Or instead, might they create stability where there is none yet? Since Forrester points out that

> there is strong indication that among real systems of importance some are unstable in the usual mathematical sense. They do not tend toward a state of static equilibrium (even in the absence of randomness or external disturbance). They are unstable, tending toward increasing amplitudes of oscillation that are contained by a continuously shifting balance of forces among the system nonlinearities. (Forrester, 1961:66)

We might take some cues from Donella Meadows when she points out that while a system's behavior is determined jointly by its parts, its inter-connections as well as its function or purpose, "changing inter-connections in a system can change it dramatically" (Meadows, 2008:17).

System Pictures

When dealing with real-time data from urban systems and networks, the SENSEable City Lab has always put as much emphasis on the research and development of adequate software platform architectures, the data analytics, as well as the communication of the information contained in the data collected and studied in the urban context. Visualizations have proven particularly useful in this undertaking. As Meadows describes so well,

> words and sentences must, by necessity, come only one at a time in linear, logical order. Systems happen all at once . . . To discuss them properly, it is necessary somehow to use a language that shares some of the same properties as the phenomena under discussion. Pictures work for this language better than words, because you can see all the parts of a picture at once. (Meadows, 2008:5)

This characteristic of being able to grasp the whole picture at once is also the reason why control rooms dealing with large amounts of data do in fact put an emphasis on diagrammatic representation rather than leaving the data in their numeric form or translating them into verbal expressions. A second reason for the strength of data visualizations is the additional processing power that can be tapped into on the spectator's side. Seeing an animated visualization of urban real-time data involves the spectator's processing power. He will bring in his prior knowledge and experience in analyzing and filtering the information in the process of observation, similar to a person standing on top of a high-rise building to observe the traffic situation before deciding in which way to drive—in this case the spectator brings in his knowledge of past dynamics and integrates them with what he sees in real-time.

Architecture for an Urban Real-Time Data Platform

From the above illustration of the overall project vision and concept, we have made an attempt to derive a platform architecture that is distinguished by two main parts: a messaging part (transporting data from a provider to a set of consumers) and a usage part. The platform is designed to handle data in the form of (real-time) data streams, which consist of an infinite sequence of messages with each message having a number of data fields. The second part of the functionality consists in data consumers being able to manipulate and process the data.

Data Transport Requirements

LIVE Singapore! has the unusual characteristic that it is not as such an application with a clearly definable use case scenario and context. It is a platform that aims at enabling a self-sustaining application development activity. We decided not to take example applications as orientation help in order to avoid slipping into customizing the platform towards a limited number of specific applications. Some cornerstones, however, must be and can be identified. LIVE Singapore! will make data streams available to the public. In the project's first phase, seven data sets and streams have been provided by government agencies, institutions and companies. The platform will also support data streams from individual devices (like smart phones) in the future. This implies that our platform needs to be able to handle a large number of data streams. For development purposes, we now assume hundreds of data streams, realizing that this number could go into the thousands.

The data streams from data providers vary widely in terms of data rates. A large telecom company partnering with us provides us with a data stream with a rate of around 300 messages per second. At the same time, the platform also has to be able to handle data streams with only a few messages per second. This is especially true if we consider individuals contributing data from their smart phones. Considering a growing number of providers in the future means that the platform is required to ultimately handle tens of thousands of messages

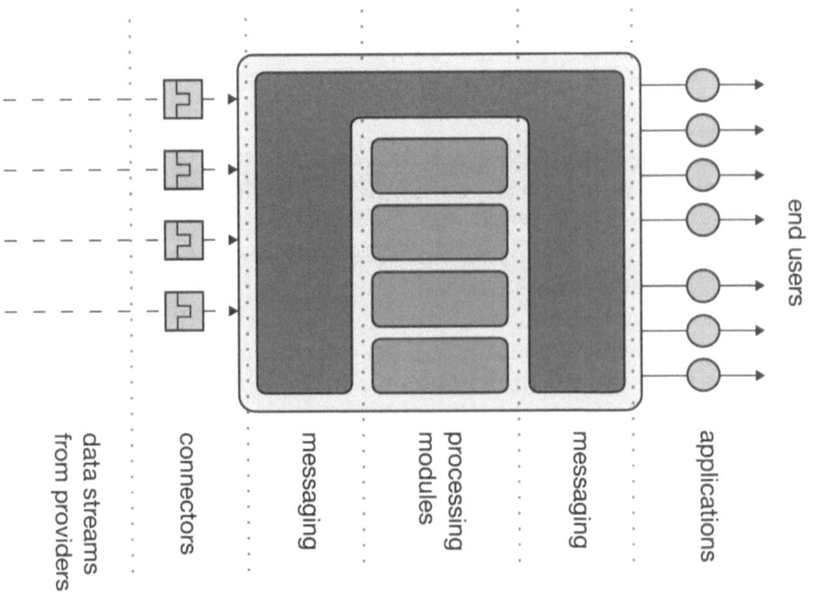

Figure 1: Platform architecture

per second in overall input load. On the output side, once the data of the platform is made publicly available, many people will be using the data (for now we assume several thousand) resulting in each data stream being distributed to a potentially large number of clients.

Taking into account the overall input load and the numbers of potential clients, and doing a quick approximation, we easily end up with up to one million messages per second. Since the initial load of the system will, however, be much smaller, it must be designed in a way to run on just a few servers initially but scale up near linearly with every server we add.

Platform Architecture

The overall architecture can best be describeSd by following messages of data streams through the platform. (See Figure 1)

Since each data provider tends to have its own data format, for data processing to become possible, the data needs to be converted into a common data format. The platform provides connectors to the data providers that allow the data to be converted into the platform data format and then forwarded to the platform (i.e., connecting to the platform messaging system).

The messaging system is then responsible for receiving the data from connectors and routing it to the client applications that need it. A client application can subscribe to individual data streams. After that, every message of that data stream is then pushed to the client.

The processing modules implement the data manipulation and processing features of the platform. They take one or several data streams as input (via the messaging system), do the processing/manipulation and output a modified data stream (to the messaging system). Client applications can then subscribe to the modified data stream in the same manner as they would for an unmodified data stream coming from a data provider (i.e., through the messaging system).

Aspects of Scalability and Flexibility

As mentioned in the requirements paragraph above, we expect that the platform will have to deal with a considerable number of messages (this causes CPU, memory, and network load). Furthermore, the processing modules impose additional load. In order to handle this load, the work has to be distributed to many machines.

While the system is designed to run on a few servers initially, it is also designed to scale up to hundreds of machines to accommodate a growing load. Our approach to achieve this scalability is that each part of the system (we call the parts components) can be run on separate machines if necessary. Each component can also be replicated on many machines if needed. Components are, for example, the individual processing modules and the parts of the messaging system.

We illustrate this by describing a common scenario: it is very likely that some particular data streams will be very popular with client applications. Many client applications will subscribe to these data streams and a single machine may not be able to distribute the messages to all the clients anymore. A component called Forwarder (See Figure 2) is then used to replicate the data stream to many machines.

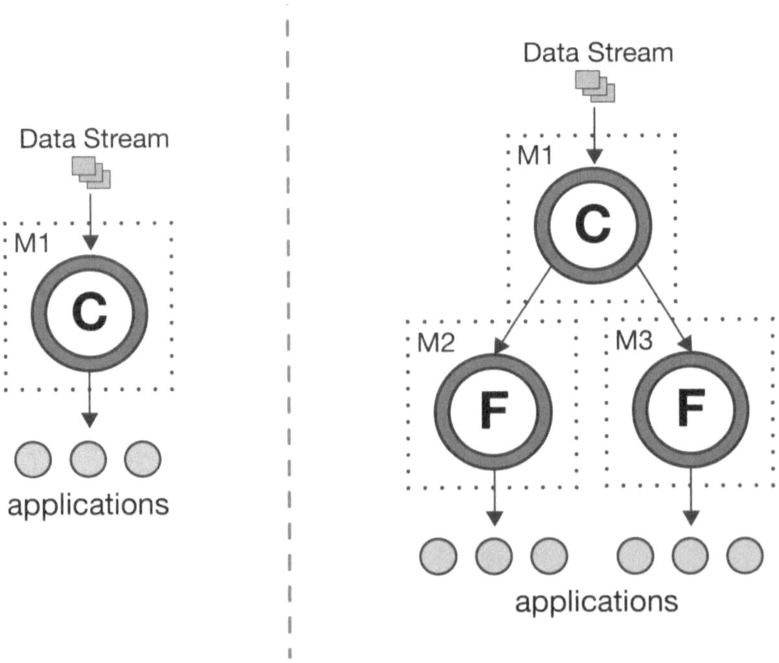

Figure 2: Forwarders replicating data stream on many machines

(In Figure 2, the data stream is replicated to two machines.) This distributes the load among two machines and enables us to support many client applications. The cost of this solution is an increased latency for messages since the messages have to be transported over one link more.

The concept works the same for other components of the system such as the processing modules. This very flexible way of running components on different machines and, therefore, distributing load works because all the components have a similar interface—they consume data from a number of data streams and output a data stream.

So far an administrator has to configure which components to run on which machines, but we plan to develop an automatic mechanism that starts and stops components depending on the current overall load of the platform and the load on individual machines.

Client applications subscribing to data-intensive data streams and/or using complex filter modules cause a heavy processing load on the platform. An advanced concept for limiting the load is to offload some of the computation to the client applications themselves. For example, the client application requesting to filter a data stream could run the filter module locally, thereby freeing platform resources.

The platform could even be outfitted with a cost model that balances computation costs and costs for transporting messages to clients. If, for example, two client applications execute the same filter over a data stream, it might be beneficial to run the filter on the platform to reduce the number of messages that need to be forwarded to the two client applications. The cost model could be made dynamic so that it considers the current platform load in terms of computation and networking load.

Data Processing Functionality

Besides transporting data from providers to consumers, LIVE Singapore! allows clients to easily process, manipulate, and visualize the data of data streams. Several modules have already been implemented in a prototype:

A Predicate Filter Module. Allows messages of data streams to be filtered. The user specifies an arbitrary complex predicate that is then evaluated for each message of a data stream (and the message is then either discarded or forwarded).

As an example, consider a data stream with a data field for humidity and temperature. The predicate could be temperature >=10 meaning that the filter would discard all messages where the temperature is below 10 degrees.

A Point-In-Polygon Filter Module. Often data streams contain geo-tagged information and many client applications may only be interested in data from a certain area. This module allows users to specify a polygon (using lat/long coordinates) and the filter then only forwards messages that have a location within that polygon.

A Truncating Module. This module allows users to remove unwanted data fields from data streams.

Our system can easily be extended with new modules. We plan to implement several modules in the future:

- A module to support "windowing" (well known from stream-processing engines). Windowing is needed, for example, when a user wants to calculate the average value of a data field for some messages. Since a data stream is an infinite sequence of messages, the user needs to be able to select a meaningful subset of the messages to calculate the average.
- A module that converts data from our internal data format to different well known formats (such as XML, CSV, JSON) requested by client applications.
- One very specific module that we would like to implement is a map-matching module that would be of great use for all transport-related data.

Since all the modules are implemented as components, they can all be linked together, allowing users to build processing chains out of simple operators. This idea is again very similar to stream-processing engines. The downside with stream-processing engines is that the operators (especially when it comes to windowing) are very complex and hard to understand and use. We plan to limit the number of modules and their functionality to make them easy to understand and use.

A second advantage of modules having data streams as outputs is that all client applications can potentially subscribe to, say, a filtered data stream created by another application. This allows users to build up a repository of useful modified data streams. Also, the platform will keep track of all the derived data streams so that we can add a mechanism that advertises popular derived data streams to users (since those are most likely meaningful ones).

A First Implementation and Evaluation of a Platform Prototype

In 2011, a first prototype of the platform was implemented. The messaging system was implemented using a low-level (TCP) messaging library called ZeroMQ

(ZeroMQ, 2011). The advantage of that library is that it allows us to implement a fast-messaging fabric both internally as well as between the platform and data providers/client applications.

The messaging system underwent some initial tests that showed that even a normal desktop machine is capable of distributing a data stream with a data rate of 1,000 messages per second to 300 clients in parallel with an average latency of around 1.3 seconds. This result shows that the overhead imposed by the messaging system is relatively low. However, many more tests will be necessary, especially to see whether scaling the messaging system works in a nearly linear manner (meaning twice the number of machines can handle almost twice the load).

Apart from the messaging part, two processing modules (predicate and point-in-polygon filters) were implemented. Also, a management console was provided allowing for the managing of the network of components that are used. Another feature of the prototype is that the new HTML 5 WebSocket protocol (WebSocket API, 2011) is supported. This means that messages of data streams can be pushed to a Web browser (or any other HTTP/HTML client). This is an important feature because, unlike the low-level TCP, it works for clients behind a firewall/NAT.

In the future, we will do a more extensive evaluation of the platform under real-world conditions and implement additional processing modules (as mentioned above). Furthermore, we plan to provide users with a toolkit that makes it easy to subscribe to data from the platform and to handle and visualize it.

Aspects of Data Format and Semantics

At the current state of the project, the data model for describing city entities and the city data is proposed to be defined using the standardized SensorML Observation and Measurement Language.

The semantic description of the city entities and all the sensory data sources is specified using the ontologies defined in the Web Ontology Language. A Domain Ontology connects all sensory data ontologies.

The semantic description of the data is decoupled from the data per se, which can instead be represented in JSON, to reduce file size and parsing overhead due to the unnecessary descriptive tags. Figure 3 shows the generation process of the data model.

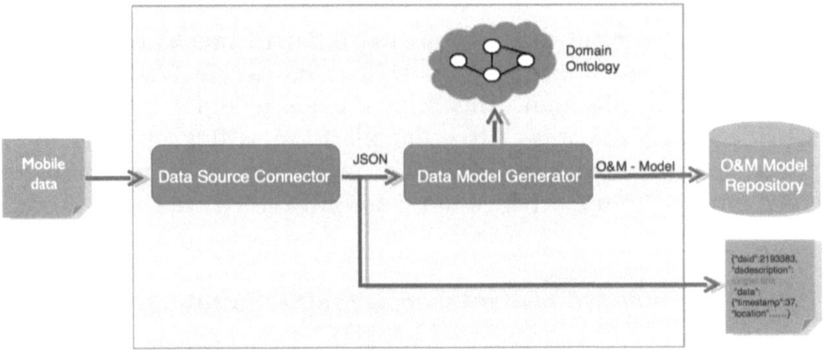

Figure 3: O&M data model generation process

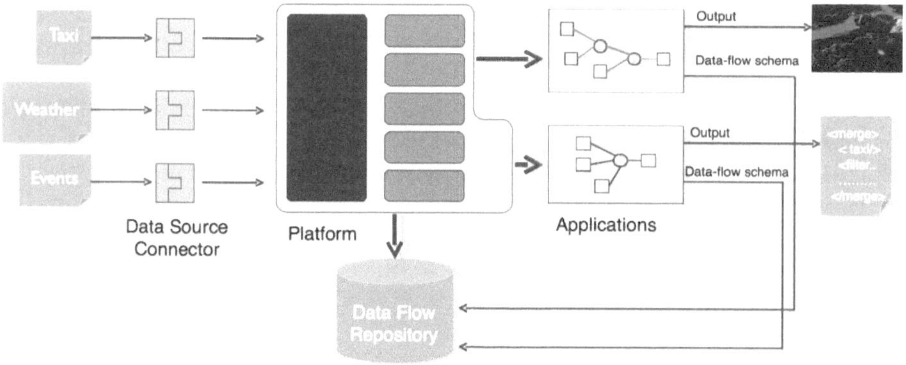

Figure 4: Central user-generated, data-flow process

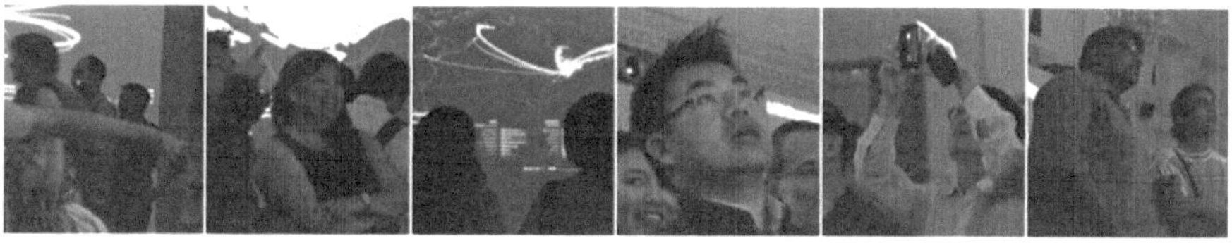

Figure 5: Photos from the LIVE Singapore! exhibition that opened April 7, 2011 at the Singapore Art Museum (SAM)

Users can use the platform to search, browse, and integrate data streams based on their semantic descriptions, and create applications. The system overview is illustrated in Figure 4. Through the platform, applications can also be published and shared among users.

LIVE Singapore! Exhibiting an Urban Demo

LIVE Singapore! is all about making real-time data available to citizens and in this spirit an exhibition was organized in April 2011 at the Singapore Art Museum. The initiative showcased some initial steps and accomplishments of the project, giving a broad audience the opportunity to engage with data generated by their city. The LIVE Singapore! exhibition, staged in the mid-nineteenth-century former Saint Joseph's Institution building, now Art museum, comprised five projections and one LCD screen showing dynamic visualizations driven by data sets and live streams from the following data providers: (See Figure 5)

- *Changi Airport Group*, operator of Singapore's airport, which is a major hub in the southeast Asian region and the seventh busiest airport in Asia by passenger traffic in 2010 (Changi Airport Group, 2012). The data set consists of the number of actual boarded passengers on all flights arriving at and departing from Changi Airport.
- *ComfortDelgro*, one of the worlds largest transport companies operating also outside of Singapore where it operates a 16,000-vehicle taxi fleet. The data set provided consists of a GPS location, the status (occupied, unoccupied, booked...), and the speed information from all taxis at irregular intervals of about one minute on average.

- *NEA*, Singapore's National Environmental Agency provided a data set indicating the rainfall across the island in terms of intensity of precipitation, derived from rain water sensors as well as radar images.
- *PSA*, operator of the port of Singapore which is the second largest container port and largest transshipment container port worldwide. The real-time data stream details all containers arriving and departing, including origin and final destination ports as well as information related to vessels' actual arrival and departure times.
- *SingTel*, Singapore's prime telecommunication company and cellphone operator. The real-time data stream provides anonymized call detail records, cellphone network usage, and cell-ID data in 15-minute intervals.
- *SP Services*, the city's electricity provider provided an aggregated data set consisting in all electrical energy consumption by commercial and industrial clients (making up 70 percent of Singapore's total electricity consumption) for each of the city's 82 postal sectors in 30-minute intervals.
- *NUS Department of Geography*, provided a public data stream from a wind speed sensor.

The exhibition setting at the Singapore Art Museum was composed of the following six visualizations, two of which offered user interaction:

Isochronic Singapore

Based on travel data from 16,000 taxis in Singapore the fastest road traffic connections are calculated and allow for the user to select an origin location. Upon this selection, the map distorts Singapore's shape to reflect the time it takes to get from the selected origin to any other part of the island. In short, if traffic is slow

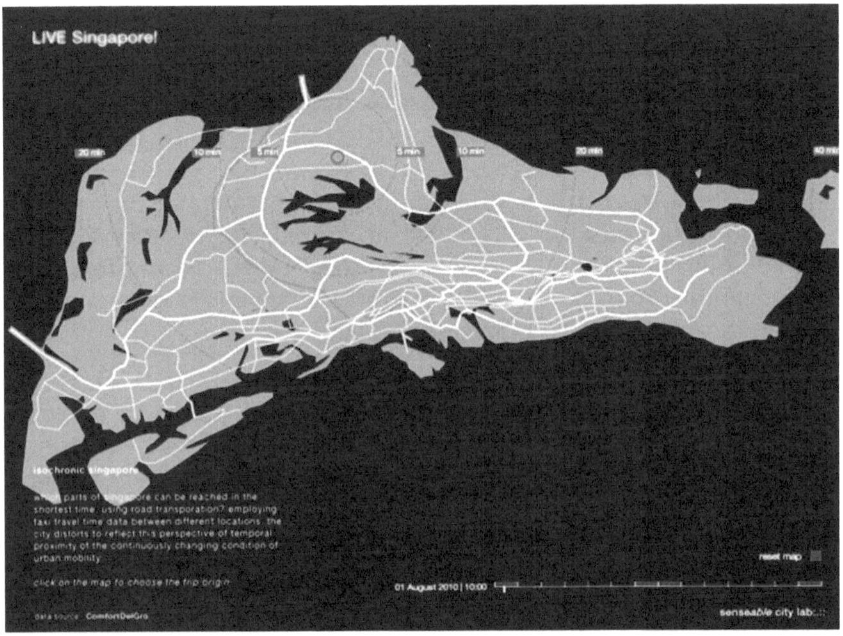

Figure 6

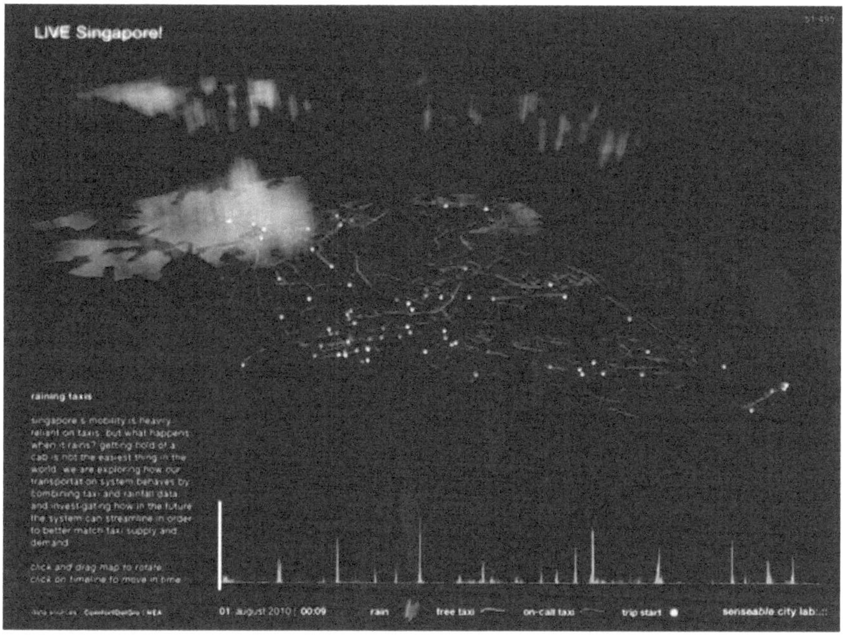

Figure 7

and travel time is long, the island grows larger while with fast traffic and shorter travel time, the island shrinks. Different areas distort differently reflecting the specific travel time to these destinations at a given time (See Figure 6).

Raining Taxis

Being located in a tropical climate, Singapore experiences frequent and often heavy rainfall of short duration that is limited to very constrained geographical areas with significant impact on transportation. This visualization brings together unoccupied taxi traces and taxi trip origins with the areas afflicted by rainfall, suggesting a multitude of possible user applications related to how to help improve supply-demand matching in high transportation demand areas caused by rainfall (See Figure 7).

Urban Heat Islands

As heat is generated by energy use, high energy consumption can translate into small local temperature rises of up to a few degrees (called man-made or anthropogenic heating). Combining data on the energy consumption of the city's different zones with the wind speed, local temperature rise can be estimated. In short, the higher the wind speed, the less local temperature rise is caused by local energy consumption due to dispersion. A potential future addition of actual measured urban temperatures will provide the basis for a future heat monitoring program (See Figure 8).

Formula One City

Large scale events disrupt a city's daily routines. Singapore's Formula One Grand Prix offers an excellent opportunity for observation. On top of a map of the city's

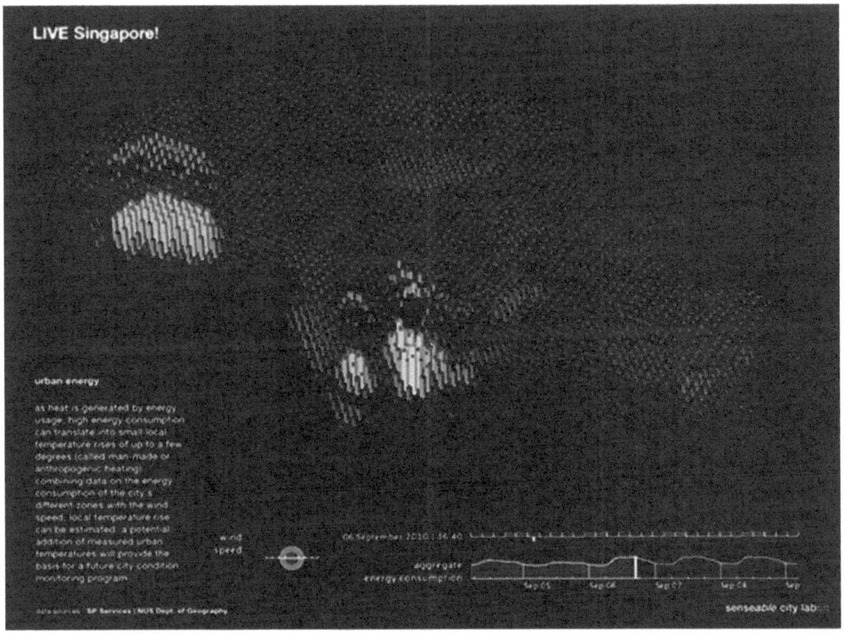

Figure 8

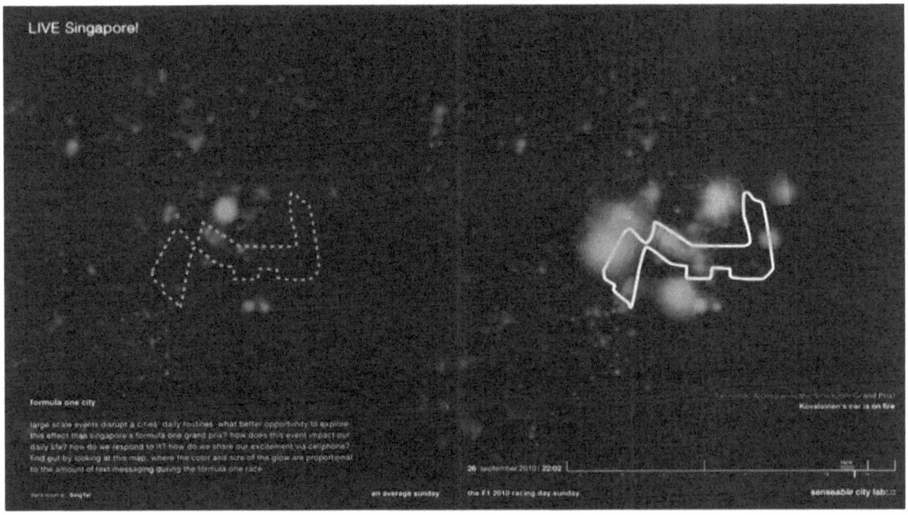

Figure 9

central district with the indicated F1 course (which in Singapore is located in the very center, composed of normal roads blocked for the event) visitors can see the network volume of SMS text messages being sent via the cellphone network antennas located in the area during a normal Sunday (on the left) and during the F1 racing Sunday in 2011. SMS text message traffic is more intense as the glow points increase in size and color intensity (See Figure 9).

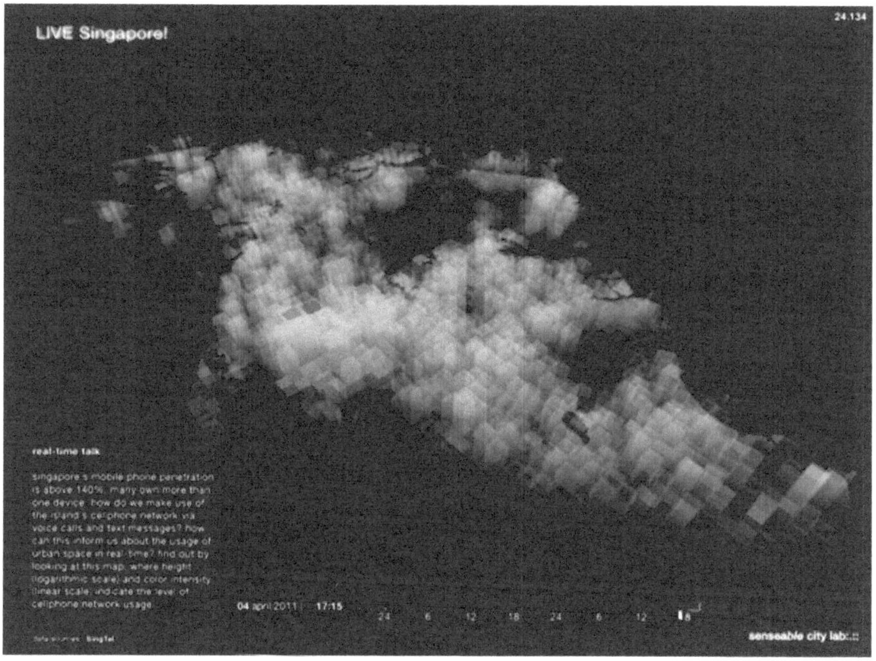

Figure 10

Real-Time Talk

Singapore's mobile phone penetration is above 140 percent, and visualizing in real-time where cellphone devices are located can give a good indication of the population distribution in urban space. The real-time data stream driving this visualization shows network call traffic intensity in terms of column height on a logarithmic scale and in terms of color intensity on a linear scale (See Figure 10).

Hub of the World

Singapore is the world's largest trans-shipment container port and one of the busiest airports in the world. Figure 11 conveys the city's role as a hub, conveying how the island is affected by the constant stream of people and goods passing through. The number of containers moving in and out from Singapore's port is represented by a line that links origin and destination of the containers and that varies in thickness according to the container number (See Figure 11).

Using the Data

The organization of the LIVE Singapore! exhibition had several purposes: Data shown in the visualizations were data generated in one way or another by people in the city. Sharing these data with the people of the city conveys the core mission of the open-platform research project. It also familiarizes and engages the city's public in critical discussion about opportunities and risks of working with urban real-time data, something we see as an important component for moving towards a real-time city. Working on the technical components of the

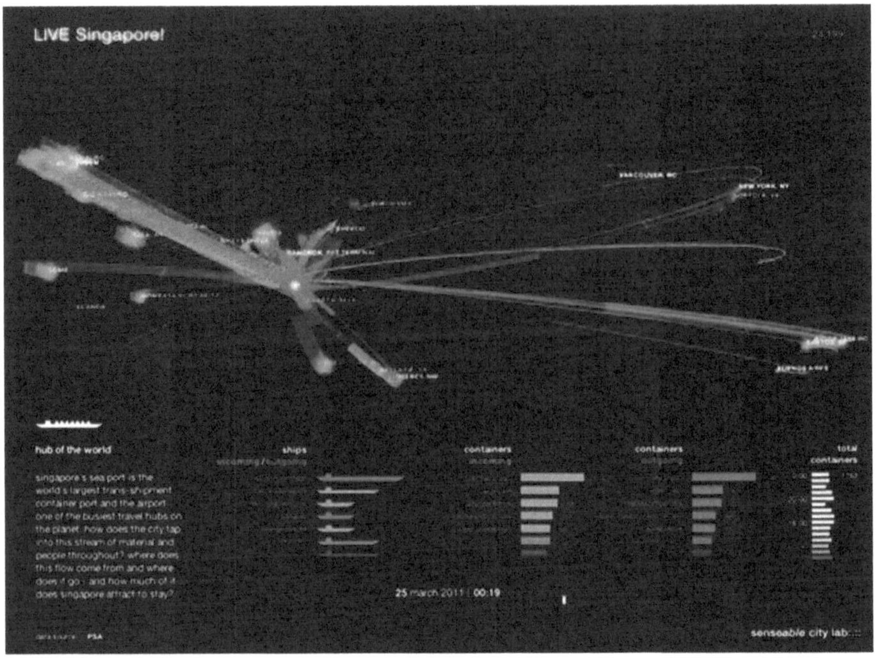

Figure 11

system has given us an exceptional opportunity to test components under real-world conditions, having to deal with a wide range of conditions and circumstances far from the theoretical concept—something certainly necessary in supporting with relevant research the development of technologies that will enable wide ranges of real-time data generated by the city's systems to be shared with its inhabitants.

Related to the domain of urban planning and management, the six real-time data visualizations described above showcase the potential for the development of applications using combinations of real-time data streams that already exist in cities. In particular, the combination of rain data and the location of free taxis in the context of a tropical climate suggests new opportunities to better accommodate high transportation demands caused by meteorological phenomena. The combination of location-specific data on electricity use and wind speed offers a contribution to the comprehensive domain of urban heat islands. And the use of taxi location data to visually represent estimations of road travel time allows for an instantaneous assessment of the road traffic situation in a specific city as well as visual comparisons among different cities.

Critical Issues

Recalling the scenario offered earlier—the description of a real-time interaction between two persons knowing each other and in a direct encounter—this scene contains a fundamental requirement indicating one of the main critical points of open data platforms such as the ones addressed in the LIVE Singapore! platform: privacy. The real-time interaction between the two figures will be the more effective the more they know about each other, be it in terms of prior knowledge or in terms of getting to know about each other as they interact. This allows each to correctly interpret the behavior of the other. In an open data platform this analogy brings up the critical notion of privacy in dealing with data collected in urban networks—data that are often directly linked to an identified citizen due to reasons of system functionality. As much as digital traces enable a system-wide awareness of urban dynamics that can constructively inform decision making in real-time, the inverse risk is what Bill Mitchell refers to as *electronic hyper-visibility*, expressing deep concern of such a reality if created without a "framework of vigilant, carefully debated, vigorously formulated and executed public policy" (Rojas, Valeri et al., 2008).

The issues of data privacy as well as data security need to be addressed in parallel with any project such as LIVE Singapore! and we have initiated an active discussion with policy makers in Singapore as well as at MIT.[1] As much as research on technical possibilities can inform policymaking, discussions on policies capable of expressing public opinion on what a society desires to do with data can and need to inform the research on the technical capabilities of a data-driven platform. While much of the public debate appears to be focused on restricting data use to ensure privacy protection, an alternative direction has been indicated by Weitzner et al. (2008) that rather proposes new forms of transparency on data use linked to clear policies on authorized uses. Over time, the issue of memory of user data has become critical when "remembering" becomes less costly than "forgetting" as Mayer-Schönberger (2011) illustrates, indicating new issues and forms of dealing with memory in the context of digital data.

At present, we have been handling data privacy within the LIVE Singapore! project by means of data aggregation and data anonymization, which have ensured concealing the identities of individuals associated with digital data streams. While effective, these approaches need to be subject to further examination regarding aspects such as the modality of aggregation (i.e., how fine or coarse does an aggregation need to be).

While the LIVE Singapore! project must, of course, be sensitive to the privacy of urban data platforms, when it is fully functioning, responsibility for the privacy of data will be more appropriately handled by the providers of the data. Considering hundreds if not thousands of data stream contributors, it is impracticable to think an open platform could handle privacy more efficiently than providers who should provide data of a kind and in a format that respects the privacy of individuals, whose information is released.

Another issue to be addressed as the platform develops will be the emergence of re-enforcing feedback in urban dynamics potentially caused by combinations of real-time data made available to citizens. When early in-car navigation devices rerouted drivers to avoid traffic jams, one consequence were secondary traffic jams on parallel roads. Will people change their decisions based on real-time information made available to them? This will be directly influenced by the way data are made available, both in terms of aspects such as delays and aggregations or combinations of data as well as the designs of interfaces by which people access that data.

A second kind of re-enforcing feedback possibly created by real-time data platforms stems from unprecedented datasets made public and combined with other data to lead to novel insights formerly unavailable to the public. An example for this would be data on the closing and opening of electricity contracts as a reflection of the behavior of the real estate market of specific neighborhoods. The public accessibility of such data could easily lead to a re-enforcement of a perceived trend and be turned into a much larger trend without any other information being available than the description of an initial state.

Aspects such as these fundamentally emerge whenever radical innovation of technology, policy, or of another kind changes the rules of how elements of the urban system connect. They need, however, be observed and studied with care in order to find their new place within that system and its modalities of interaction.

Where Are We and What Is Next?

The LIVE Singapore! project is a five-year research initiative started in mid 2010 and has reached the following state: a platform prototype has been implemented as outlined above, allowing at present the development of applications on top of the platform that is at this stage operating internally.

In April 2011, the LIVE Singapore! exhibition was staged at the Singapore Art Museum in which we showcased six applications developed within the LIVE Singapore! framework that combined multiple real-time streams, making them accessible to the public by means of visualizations (some of which allow user interaction) of the data that gave insights into the city's dynamics as they happened and demonstrated the usefulness of real-time data in concrete urban contexts. These applications were realized with data streams coming from an initial group of data sharing partners.

On the basis of these developments several conclusions can already be drawn that are informing the next steps of the project's development:

- It emerged in the collaboration with all partners sharing data with the platform that they had to make a major effort to prepare the data to be shared. The effort is manifold and some of the core points include: ensuring data privacy, extrapolating relevant and non-sensitive fields as well as structuring the data in a coherent format. This confirms the common idea of the existence of "data silos"—highly developed data systems where data are difficult to combine—these systems have not been set up with the purpose of sharing operational data with an external entity such as an open urban data platform. The process of interacting with our initial partners will substantially inform the formulation of standard procedures, policies, and data structures for the next phase of the platform, keeping in mind the above outlined contrasting objectives of a high level of data coherence as well as reduced requirements of data preparation by the providers. On the positive side, however, is the high level of commitment by the data-sharing partners who are motivated to address these issues, indicating an awareness of the overall benefit of an urban data platform such as LIVE Singapore! In some cases, the project has been taken by partners as a stimulus to address internal data incoherences and incompatibilities—an effort that will prove useful both for work done with data within the single network as well as preparing it for combined uses such as within the LIVE Singapore! platform framework.

- It is difficult to formulate data sharing partnerships such as LIVE Singapore! Our experience in Singapore has been very encouraging because we found highly motivated and cooperative partners but through the program, we have also enhanced our understanding of the necessity to formulate a clear incentive framework for an urban real-time data platform. Simply put: what is the incentive for any one data provider to provide its data to such a platform? And how is it possible to ignite the process when the full potential is unleashed only when there are numerous such data contributors? Again, the experience in Singapore suggests that there is an increased awareness among institutions and companies that the combination of their data with other data sources holds compelling potential, and sharing their data in order to have access to data shared by others is starting to be perceived as a viable approach. Some current data-sharing partners of LIVE Singapore! have expressed interest in sharing some of their data publicly; they have spoken of setting aside certain other data sets on a "reserved" part of the platform. These suggestions have led us to consider modifying the design of the platform's structure.

- Singapore is a lively business environment and we have seen an eagerness to take a project such as LIVE Singapore quickly towards a city-wide implementation level and explore new business opportunities that this would open up. While such an implementation will require further research and development, it does anticipate the mandatory question of a viable and sustainable business model for a platform such as LIVE Singapore! Will data be made available free of charge by the providers? Shall resulting applications be without charge too? If developers charge for applications that make use of several real-time feeds, will the data providers participate in the earnings? And finally what kind of entity (private, public...) would best be indicated to operate the platform which at present is managed within our academic research group?

A key aspect of the next steps of LIVE Singapore! will be "accessibility." After the initial phase of laying the basis and developing a working prototype of the platform architecture, activating real-world, real-time feeds together with our partners as well as programming first applications on top of this framework, LIVE Singapore!'s explicit emphasis is on creating easy access for external data providers as well as easy access to developers and users of the city's real-time streams and allowing for the programmability of these. A second main aspect will be the involvement of other forms of data contribution to the platform such as user generated data. This will bring up the issues of data reliability when moving outside acknowledged institutionalized reliability measures. It will also bring up the opportunity of such a platform in allowing the city's inhabitants to determine new kinds of data to be created that go beyond the existing bits that are generated by existing infrastructures, in this way representing an active and direct involvement of citizens in exploring the future of programming the city.

Note

1. SENSEable City Lab in 2009 organized the "Engaging Data Forum" with the objective of exploring the novel applications for electronic data and addressing the risks, concerns, and consumer opinions associated with the use of these data.

Note on Contributors

Kristian Kloeckl is a research scientist at the Senseable City Lab at the Massachusetts Institute of Technology and is the project leader of the LIVE Singapore! project.

Oliver Senn is a senior research engineer at the Singapore-MIT Alliance for Technology.

Carlo Ratti is director of the Senseable City Lab at the Massachusetts Institute of Technology and is the principal investigator of the LIVE Singapore! project.

Bibliography

F. Calabrese, M. Colonna, P. Lovisolo, D. Parata, and C. Ratti, "Real-Time Urban Monitoring Using Cell Phones: A Case-Study in Rome," *IEEE Transactions on Intelligent Transportation Systems* 12:1 (2011) 141–151.

F. Calabrese and C. Ratti, "Real Time Rome," Networks and Communication Studies: Official Journal of the IGU's Geography of Information Society Commission 20:3-4 (2006) 247–258.

F. Calabrese, K. Kloeckl, and C. Ratti, "Wikicity: Real-Time Location-Sensitive Tools for the City," paper presented at *Computers in Urban Planning and Urban Management* (Iguassu Falls, July 11–13, 2007).

Changi Airport Group, *About Changi Airport* (2012) <http://www.changiairport.com/our-business/about-changi-airport;jsessionid=C922B544B9134D218744AC97A78131D4>

data.gov <http://www.data.gov/about> Accessed January 3, 2011.

M. Foth, N. Odendaal, and G. Hearn, "The View from Everywhere: Towards an Epistemology for Urbanites," paper presented at the 4th International Conference on Intellectual Capital, Knowledge Management and Organizational Learning (Cape Town, South Africa, 2007).

J. Forrester, *Industrial Dynamics* (Cambridge, MA: MIT Press, 1961).

C. Henson, A. Sheth, and S. Sahoo, "Semantic Sensor Web," *IEEE Internet Computing* 12:4 (2008) 78–83.

IDA Singapore, *Telecommunications Report* (2012) <http://www.ida.gov.sg/Publications/20070822130650.aspx> Accessed 30 March, 2012.

ITU, *The Internet of Things*, Report of the International Telecommunication Union (Geneva, 2005).

V. Mayer-Schönberger, *The Virtue of Forgetting in the Digital Age* (Princeton: Princeton University Press, 2011).

D. Meadows, *Thinking in Systems: A Primer* (White River Junction, VT: Chelsea Green, 2008).

R. Murty, G. Mainland, I. Rose, A. Chowdhury, A. Gosain, J. Bers, and M. Welsh, "CitySense: A Vision for an Urban-Scale Wireless Networking Testbed," paper presented at IEEE International Conference on Technologies for Homeland Security (Waltham, MA, May 12–13, 2008).

Open Geospatial Consortium <http://www.opengeospatial.org> Accessed March 30, 2012. *Oxford English Dictionary* (Oxford: Oxford University Press, 2007).

Pachube <http://www,pachube,com/> Accessed March 1, 2011.

Paulsen, H. and Riegger, U. (2006) "SensorGIS - Geodaten in Echtzeit," In: *GIS-Business* (April 2006).

F. Rojas, K. Kloeckl, and C. Ratti, "Dynamic City, Investigations into the Sensing, Analysis and Application of Real-time, Location-based Data," paper presented at the First International Conference on Critical Digital: What Matters(s)?, (Cambridge, MA, April 18–19, 2008).

F. Rojas, C. Valeri, K. Kloeckl, and C. Ratti, *New York Talk Exchange* (Cambridge, MA: SA+P Press, 2008).

Singapore Department of Statistics, *Time Series on Annual GDP at Current Market Prices* (2012) <http://www.singstat.gov.sg/stats/themes/economy/hist/gdp2.html Accessed July 2012.

Singapore Land Transport, *Statistics in Brief* (2012) <http://www.lta.gov.sg/content/dam/lta/Corporate/doc/LTA-Stats%20in%20Brief%202012_C.pdf> Accessed July 2012.

M. Taylor, *The Moment of Complexity: Emerging Network Culture* (Chicago: University of Chicago Press, 2001).

W3C, *OWL: Web Ontology Language* (2004) <http://www.w3.org/TR/owl-features/> Accessed March 30, 2012.

W3C, *WebSocket API* <http://dev.w3.org/html5/websockets/> Accessed March 30, 2012.

D. Weitzner, H. Abelson, T. Berners-Lee, J. Feigenbaum, J. Hendler, and G. Sussman, "Information Accountability," *Communications of the ACM* 51:6 (2008) 82–87.

Yahoo Pipes <http://pipes,yahoo,com/pipes/> Accessed March 1, 2011.

M. Zardini, ed., *Sense of the City: An Alternate Approach to Urbanism* (Baden, Switzerland: Lars Müller, 2006).

ZeroMQ <http://www.zeromq.org/> Accessed March 3, 2011.

Index

Page numbers in **bold** type refer to figures
Page numbers in *italic* type refer to tables
Page numbers followed by 'n' refer to notes